The
Illustrated World of
Wild Animals

The
Illustrated World of
Wild Animals

Mark Carwardine

TED SMART

For my grandmother, Kathleen Carwardine

Barn owl

This edition was published for
The Book People
Guardian House
Borough Road
Godalming Surrey GU7 2AE

Copyright © 1988 Ilex Publishers Limited

Designed by Designers and Partners, Oxford
Illustrated by Jim Channell, Martin Camm, Dick Twinney and John Francis
courtesy of Bernard Thornton Artists.

Created and produced by Ilex Publishers Limited,
29-31 George Street, Oxford OX1 2AJ

ISBN 1-85613-039-8

Printed in Spain

CONTENTS

INTRODUCTION

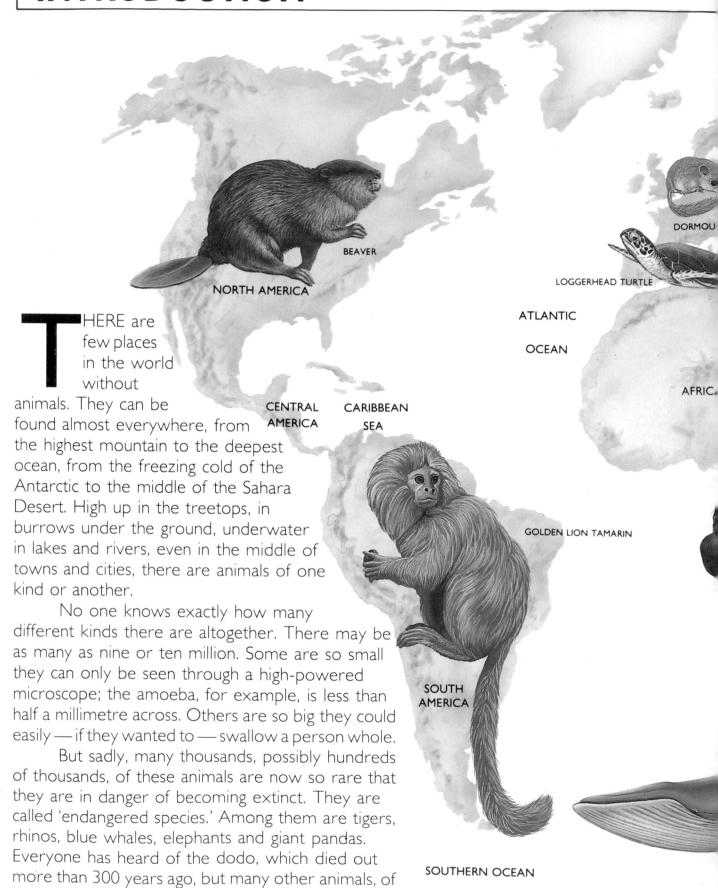

BEAVER

NORTH AMERICA

DORMOU

LOGGERHEAD TURTLE

ATLANTIC

OCEAN

AFRIC

CENTRAL AMERICA   **CARIBBEAN SEA**

GOLDEN LION TAMARIN

SOUTH AMERICA

SOUTHERN OCEAN

THERE are few places in the world without animals. They can be found almost everywhere, from the highest mountain to the deepest ocean, from the freezing cold of the Antarctic to the middle of the Sahara Desert. High up in the treetops, in burrows under the ground, underwater in lakes and rivers, even in the middle of towns and cities, there are animals of one kind or another.

No one knows exactly how many different kinds there are altogether. There may be as many as nine or ten million. Some are so small they can only be seen through a high-powered microscope; the amoeba, for example, is less than half a millimetre across. Others are so big they could easily — if they wanted to — swallow a person whole.

But sadly, many thousands, possibly hundreds of thousands, of these animals are now so rare that they are in danger of becoming extinct. They are called 'endangered species.' Among them are tigers, rhinos, blue whales, elephants and giant pandas. Everyone has heard of the dodo, which died out more than 300 years ago, but many other animals, of all shapes and sizes, have become extinct since then. Some scientists believe that 1,000 endangered species or more are dying out every year.

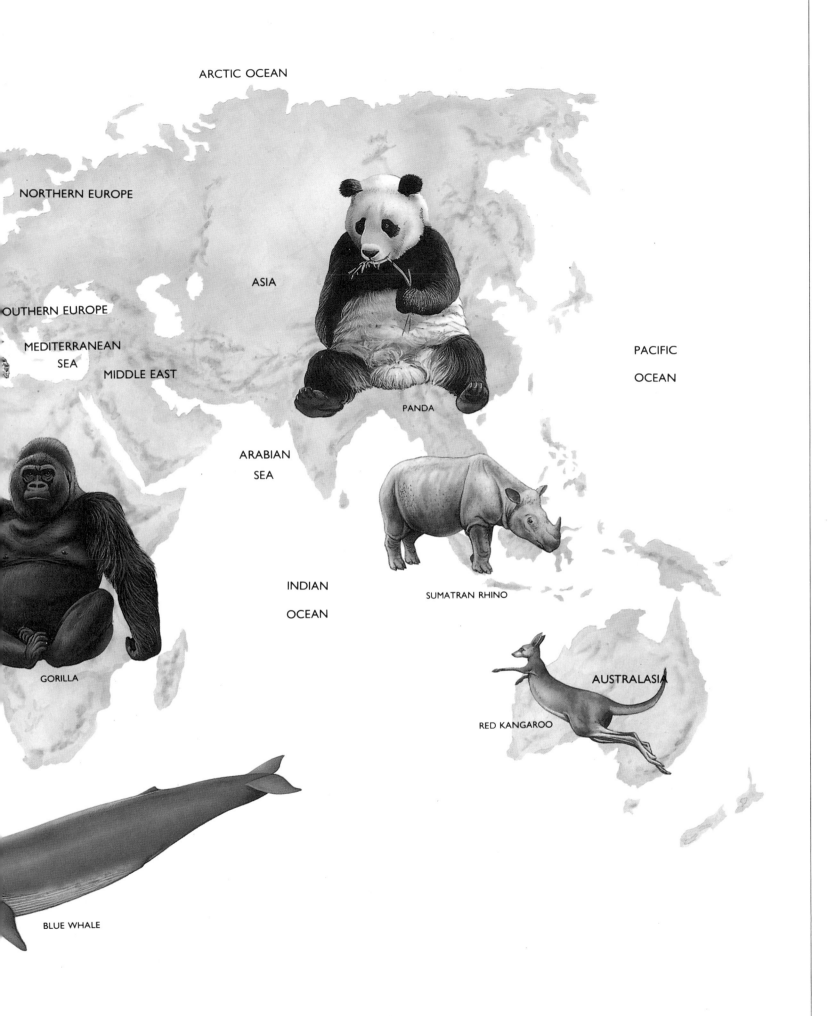

ARCTIC OCEAN

NORTHERN EUROPE

ASIA

OUTHERN EUROPE

MEDITERRANEAN
SEA

MIDDLE EAST

PACIFIC

OCEAN

PANDA

ARABIAN
SEA

SUMATRAN RHINO

INDIAN

OCEAN

GORILLA

AUSTRALASIA

RED KANGAROO

BLUE WHALE

NORTHERN EUROPE

GREENLAND

Nightingale
The nightingale's song is one of the most beautiful sounds of the countryside. Loud, clear and endlessly variable, it has been the subject of many poems over the centuries. Although the nightingale sings only during spring and early summer, it can be heard at night as well as during the day.

Red squirrel
Red squirrels feed mostly on the seeds of pine cones, sometimes while hanging upside down from a branch. A single squirrel can get through as many as one hundred and fifty cones a day, taking about three minutes to remove and eat all the seeds from each one.

Frog
Frogs are famous for their leaping abilities. They leap to get from one place to another, or to escape from their enemies. They often disappear so quickly that they are almost impossible to catch.

ICELAND

NORTH ATLANTIC OCEAN

NORTHERN IRELAND

SCOTLAND

REPUBLIC OF IRELAND

NORTH SEA

WALES   ENGLAND

NORWAY

SWEDEN

FINLAND

DENMARK

BALTIC SEA

U.S.S.R.
(UNION OF SOVIET
SOCIALIST REPUBLICS)

NETHERLANDS

EAST GERMANY

BELGIUM

WEST GERMANY

POLAND

LUXEMBOURG

CZECHOSLOVAKIA

FRANCE

AUSTRIA

HUNGARY

ROMANIA

Flying squirrel
Flying squirrels look rather like normal squirrels, when they are clinging to a tree trunk or running through the treetops. But when a branch or tree is too far away to reach with an ordinary leap, they behave quite differently.

They climb as high as they can and then fling themselves into the air. A special piece of skin between their arms and legs acts like the wings of a glider and they float from the top of one tree to the trunk of the next.

Mole
Moles spend almost their entire lives in tunnels under the ground. They dig these themselves with their front feet. The loose soil they push to the surface during digging forms the tell-tale mole hills.

Woodpecker
There are over two hundred different kinds of woodpeckers around the world. They have sharply clawed feet – for clinging tightly to tree trunks – and strong, straight beaks for hammering out their nesting holes or to get at tasty insects under the bark.

Osprey
The osprey is an expert fisherman. It flies over a lake or river to look for a suitable trout or pike near the surface. Then it plunges into the water with a big splash – often going right under – and grabs the surprised fish with both its feet.

Otter
Otters are very playful animals. They love sliding around in the snow, somersaulting, blowing bubbles, chasing their tails and even balancing stones on their heads.

Red fox
Foxes are common animals in towns and cities in many parts of the world and even make their dens, or 'earths', under garden sheds or in the middle of dense flower beds. They eat virtually anything – from small deer and grasshoppers to earthworms and dustbin scraps.

N ORTHERN EUROPE covers only about two per cent of the world's land area. Yet it is very densely populated and, over the centuries, its inhabitants have had a tremendous influence on other countries. Their different cultures, languages and traditions have reached into the lives of people all over the world.

Stretching from Greenland in the north, high above the Arctic Circle, to Switzerland in the south, northern Europe contains about 20 different countries. It also includes nearly a quarter of Russia – though the vast region beyond the Ural mountains and Caspian Sea belongs to Asia.

OSPREY

RED SQUIRREL

LEMMING

SWIFT

OTTER

HARVEST MOUSE

NIGHTJAR

GRASS SNAKE

TAWNY OWL

RED FOX

MOLE

PIPISTRELLE BAT

HEDGEHOG

NIGHTINGALE

Hedgehog

The hedgehog's back is covered with about 5,000 spines. These are modified hairs which are important for protection. When threatened, the hedgehog simply rolls up into a tight and spiny ball. It can stay like this for hours – and there is no way another animal, like a badger or a fox, can get in.

A long winter sleep

DORMICE live mostly in woods, hedgerows and gardens and scramble about in the trees and bushes with great agility. They are famous for their long winter sleep, which lasts for seven months or more. Curled up, they look like tiny balls of fur, hidden in special nests under leaves or moss, or in a rotten log.

In preparation for this long sleep, they begin stuffing themselves with food in the early autumn. They eat as many nuts and seeds and as much fruit as they can.

By the time they are ready for winter, they are so fat that they have nearly doubled in weight.

During their sleep, or hibernation, they live off this stored fat. By the time they wake up in the spring they are much, much thinner – so the first thing the dormice do on waking is to search for more food!

Much of northern Europe was originally covered with forest. But over the years most of the trees have been chopped down and replaced with farmland and towns and cities. Sadly, as the countryside disappears, there are fewer places for plants and animals to live. Some species, like badgers and foxes, have been able to adapt to living in parks and gardens. Others, like the Scottish wild cat, have retreated and now live only in very remote areas far away from people. Many species have disappeared altogether – because they have nowhere left to live, or because they were hunted to extinction.

Wolves and wild boars used to be common animals in Britain, but they became extinct many years ago; and the world's last pair of great auks was killed in Iceland in 1844.

North European plants and animals are still becoming extinct today. despite thousands of nature

Blue whale

The blue whale is the largest animal in the world. Weighing more than thirty elephants – about 150 tonnes – and measuring up to 30 metres in length, it is even bigger than the largest of all the dinosaurs. Blue whales are found in all the world's oceans but are now very rare.

The Loch Ness Monster

IS there really a prehistoric animal still living in Scotland? Many people believe there is one – perhaps even a colony of them – alive and well in Loch Ness. Many even claim to have seen 'Nessie', as the 'monster' has become known, and have taken photographs of strange shapes in the water. On a few occasions it has even been reported actually out of the water!

Loch Ness is certainly big enough to hide such a creature. It is about 40 kilometres long and up to three kilometres wide. A third of the loch is over 175 metres deep; and it is full of large fish, such as salmon, trout and pike, so there would be plenty for Nessie to eat.

There are also reports of other strange 'monsters' from many parts of the world. People claim to have seen giant octopuses and sea serpents, huge snow-men and monstrous plants. These sightings are all being investigated by scientists but many people are very suspicious and think it is unlikely that such creatures really do exist.

However, no-one believed that reports of an animal which looked like a cross between a zebra and a giraffe were true – until the strange-looking okapi was discovered in the jungles of West Africa in 1901. So there is still a possibility that Nessie and some of the other 'monsters' really do exist, after all.

Longest animals in the world

maximum recorded (metres)

Mammals:
blue whale
27.60

Birds:
wandering albatross (wing span)
3.63

Reptiles:
reticulated python
10.00

Amphibians:
chinese water salamander
1.80

Fish:
whale shark
18.50

Invertebrates:
bootlace worm
55.00

Nightjar
After dark, when most other birds are asleep, the nightjar wheels and twists in the air, using its mouth like a butterfly net. The mouth is so big that it can catch anything from a small swarm of mosquitos to a giant moth.

reserves and national parks to protect them. The large blue butterfly, for example, disappeared from Britain as recently as 1979.

But northern Europe still has a rich collection of wildlife and wild places. There are spectacular bird cliffs – with puffins, guillemots, gannets and razorbills – and otters, sea eagles, golden eagles, flamingos, chamois and many other exciting species.

Salmon are famous for their dangerous journeys up rivers to lay their eggs. They often have to swim against powerful currents and leap as high as five metres over waterfalls, in order to return to exactly the same spot in the river where they themselves hatched. After breeding, most of the adult salmon die before they can complete the journey back to sea.

Some of the deepest caves in the world are to be found in France and Austria; Greenland – the world's largest island – has one of the longest glaciers; and there are dramatic waterfalls, active volcanos and beautiful mountain ranges in Norway, Iceland, Switzerland and many other countries.

Why do so many lemmings die?

THERE are many stories about lemmings marching to the sea in their thousands and drowning themselves. But they never *try* to get killed – and there are good reasons for taking all the risks involved in their dangerous journeys.

Every three or four years, lemming numbers increase so much that many of the animals are forced out of their homes. When there is not enough space, fights often break out until some decide to leave. Once they are on the move – looking for somewhere else to live – they are so determined that nothing can stop them. But many die from exhaustion or starvation; some are eaten by predators. Others are drowned while they try to cross big or dangerous rivers – or by trying to swim across the sea, not realising how big it is.

Animals of the night

BADGERS spend the daytime sleeping underground, in a sett. A typical badger sett is a jungle of tunnels and rooms, with many entrances, used by up to ten or more of the animals. The rooms, or chambers, are lined with heaps of bedding, consisting mostly of leaves and grass, which the badgers drag in on dry nights.

The badgers cautiously emerge from their setts at dusk, or during the night. At first, they sniff the air for any sign of danger. Then, when they are sure it is safe, they stand outside one of the holes to give themselves a good scratch. Very occasionally, in remoter areas, they will come out earlier and can be seen in broad daylight. Most people who are lucky enough to see badgers, however, see them at night caught in a car's headlights as they amble across the road.

Tawny owl
Tawny owls are familiar birds to many people, as they often live in towns and cities. Although they come out at night, their well-known hooting always gives their presence away. Legend has it that the owl is a wise bird – perhaps because its large eyes stare forward like a person – but as birds go, it is not particularly bright.

DID YOU KNOW?

One pipistrelle bat, which is about the size of a mouse, can eat up to 3,500 insects in a single night.

If threatened, the European grass snake will play dead by opening its mouth and letting its tongue droop out.

The correct name for a group of crows is a 'murder'.

The young caterpillars of the swallowtail butterfly resemble bird droppings and therefore escape being eaten by too many of their predators.

The fastest animal in the world is the peregrine falcon, which has been known to reach 350 kilometres per hour during one of its aerial hunting dives.

A leech can 'drink' up to five times its own weight in blood at one sitting of just a few hours. But it may take several months to digest the meal. If a leech lands on your arm or leg, you may not feel it at all – it anaesthetises your skin before beginning its meal.

A group of geese on the ground is called a 'gaggle' – but as soon as the birds take to the air they become known as a 'skein', often flying in a characteristic V-formation.

Non-stop flight

SWIFTS spend most of their lives in the air. They fly non-stop from the moment they leave their nests to the day they begin building nests of their own. By the time they land for the first time, they have been flying for up to three years and have travelled over half a million kilometres.

Swifts sleep and eat in the air. Their long wings help them to glide and fly, wheeling and turning for hours on end. Sometimes they fly hundreds of kilometres in a single day while feeding, catching insects with their enormous beaks.

Swifts are among the fastest-flying birds in the world. The white-throated spinetail swift is the overall record-holder, able to reach speeds of 170 kilometres an hour.

Harvest mouse

The harvest mouse is like a little grassland monkey. It spends a great deal of its time scrambling around in the tops of grass stems and other stiff-stalked vegetation. An excellent climber, it even has a tail like a monkey, which can be curled around a stalk and can easily hold the animal's weight.

SOUTHERN EUROPE

SOUTHERN EUROPE is tiny compared with the other regions of the earth, like North America and Africa. It consists of only fifteen countries. One of these – Vatican City – is the smallest nation in the world. Surrounded by Rome, it is only 44 hectares in size. Another small member country is Turkey. Only a minute part of it – in the extreme west – is considered European. The rest is in Asia.

Most countries in southern Europe are clustered around the Mediterranean. Their coastlines are very jagged and irregular, making strange shapes in the sea. Italy, for example, is shaped like a boot. There are also many islands, such as Malta, Corfu, Majorca, Zakynthos and Corsica.

Spanish lynx
The Spanish lynx is rarely seen. It comes out at night and, when prowling around in its forest and scrubland home, is always alert. It can see and hear extremely well and can always tell when danger is approaching. Then it quickly hides, crouching down in the nearest cover until the danger has passed.

Flamingo
When they are feeding, flamingos hold their heads upside-down in the water. They suck in mud and water through their bills and filter out all the tiny plants and animals trapped inside.

ATLANTIC OCEAN

SWITZERLAND

FRANCE

SPAIN

PORTUGAL

MEDITERRANEAN SEA

ITAL

GIBRALTAR

Are there any monkeys in Europe?

MOST monkeys and their relatives are found in South America, Africa and Asia. But there is also a famous colony which lives on the Rock of Gibraltar, in southern Europe.

No one is really sure how these bright and adaptable monkeys came to be on the Rock. But it seems quite likely that they were taken there – from North Africa – by the Romans.

These days there are between thirty and forty of them, living in two separate groups, or troops. Also known as barbary apes – though they are not apes at all – they are completely free and spend much of their time foraging for roots and berries. But they are also fed twice every day by an officer of the Gibraltar Regiment.

Water vole
Water voles live along the plant-covered banks of rivers, ponds and canals. These rat-sized, shaggy little animals spend their lives eating grass and rushes. They are more often heard than seen, as they 'plop' into the water and disappear underneath.

Spanish ibex
The Spanish ibex is a kind of wild goat. A very rare animal, it lives on the rocky crags and steep cliffs of some of the most rugged mountainous areas in Spain. A difficult animal to see, it is active mostly in the late afternoon and throughout moonlit nights. Like other mountain goats, it is an expert at climbing and jumping.

Pikas
Pikas usually live in rather remote areas, away from people. They are very noisy animals, always barking or bleating at one another.

Wolf
Wolves keep in touch with one another by howling. The 'lonesome howl' may mean that an animal has become separated from its pack. But very often the whole pack howls together — to warn other wolves to stay away, or to call their friends together after a hunt.

YUGOSLAVIA

BULGARIA

ALBANIA

TURKEY

GREECE

CYPRUS

Brown bear
Brown bears vary enormously in size. The animals found in southern Europe are among the smallest in the world; some of the North American individuals are more than four times as big. These larger 'grizzlies' sometimes feed on animals the size of bison and moose — even, on occasion, black bears. But the smaller individuals prefer grasses, moss, roots, berries, bulbs and small mammals.

Mediterranean monk seal
The Mediterranean monk seal is one of the rarest seals in the world. Hunters and fishermen have killed large numbers of them and they have been frightened away from their favourite sandy beaches by tourists. Now there are fewer than five hundred of the animals left.

15

The Mediterranean is the third largest sea in the world – after the South China and Caribbean Seas – and home to many different kinds of wildlife. There are, among other south European specialities, monk seals and loggerhead turtles in the water; and Spanish lynx, brown bears and white storks on the land.

Migration

GREY whales, salmon, locusts, wildebeest, lemmings, monarch butterflies and many other animals make regular migrations. They travel from one place to another to find food or water, to breed in more suitable places, to avoid bad weather or even because their original homes are too crowded.

Birds are perhaps the best-known of all migrants. Nearly half all the birds in the world are migratory.

Incredibly, they fly thousands of kilometres – every spring and autumn – while navigating by the stars or by landmarks such as coastlines or rivers. Most fly at heights below about 2,000 metres but some geese have been seen crossing the Himalayas – at a height of more than 9,500 metres.

Several hundred bird species fly over Europe during their annual travels. There are some outstanding places in southern Europe, such as Istanbul and Gibraltar, where enormous numbers of them – including storks, buzzards, eagles, kites and falcons – can be seen travelling between Europe and Africa.

Genet
Genets hunt mainly at night. They spend the daytime sleeping, curled up in a hollow tree, under a bush, or in tall grass. Their blotched fur blends in perfectly with the surroundings and makes them almost invisible.

Grey whale
up to 20,000km/ year between the Arctic Ocean and Mexico

Wild boar

The wild boar is the only wild member of the pig family found in Europe. It disappeared from Britain about 300 years ago but still occurs in many countries on mainland Europe. Like other pigs, wild boars love wallowing in mud pools. As well as being fun, the mud cools them off and gets rid of all their insect pests.

But the wildlife of southern Europe is not as rich as it once was. Before people arrived in the area there were forests, long stretches of natural coastline and clean seawater. Today the forests have been chopped down, rows and rows of hotels and other buildings stretch for hundreds of kilometres along the coast and the sea is polluted with oil and sewage. But despite all this destruction some of the world's most outstanding natural areas are still to be found in southern Europe.

Lesser kestrels naturally breed on cliff ledges – but they have happily taken to building their nests on the 'man-made cliffs' provided by window ledges, roofs, cathedral towers and derelict buildings.

Migration distances

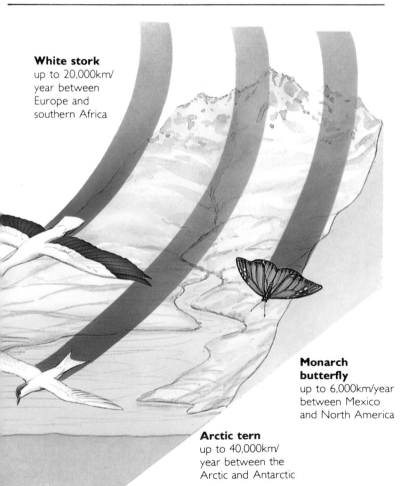

White stork
up to 20,000km/ year between Europe and southern Africa

Monarch butterfly
up to 6,000km/year between Mexico and North America

Arctic tern
up to 40,000km/ year between the Arctic and Antarctic

Mountain climbers

THE chamois is a daring, agile and graceful animal. It is famous for its incredible sense of balance and breathtaking leaps. About the size of a goat, it can easily jump four metres high and over six metres across.

Chamois are found in the dangerous mountainous country of central and southern Europe. More sure-footed and nimble than any mountaineer could ever hope to be, there are very few places which they cannot reach by climbing or jumping.

Young chamois learn their mountaineering skills very quickly. After a few practice jumps on and off their mothers' backs, they happily follow the rest of the herd wherever it goes.

17

There are famous volcanos such as Vesuvius, near Naples, and Etna, in Sicily; rich wildlife reserves like Spain's Coto Donana and the Camargue, in France; beautiful waterfalls, as in Plitvice National Park, Yugoslavia; and spectacular mountain ranges such as the Pyrenees and the Alps.

The clacking sound of spring

IN many parts of Europe, the first indication that spring has arrived is a loud clacking noise. It is made by white storks arriving from Africa. As they soar high above a town or village, floating on bands of rising warm air (called thermals) they clack their bright-red bills together so loudly that they can be heard long before they are seen.

White storks nest on chimney stacks and roofs. Year after year they return to exactly the same spots to build their nests. In many towns people erect cartwheels and other platforms to help the birds find a suitable base. They use such enormous masses of nesting material that house sparrows often build their nests inside. A single stork nest may contain a dozen or more nesting sparrows.

White storks have been protected in Europe for centuries. But their numbers are dwindling. They have already disappeared from Sweden, Switzerland and some other countries, and only a few dozen are left in many others.

MANY animals avoid the need to hunt by feeding on prey that has already been killed or has died from other causes. These 'lazy predators' – vultures are perhaps the most famous – are known as scavengers.

If a circling vulture spots a dead animal it quickly descends to a nearby tree and then drops to the ground. Any neighbouring vultures seeing the first bird

Golden hamster
Golden hamsters are very popular as pets but are also common animals in the wild. Found in many parts of Europe and Asia, they live along riverbanks, in fields, in deserts and even on mountain slopes. They have enormous pouches in their cheeks, which are used like shopping baskets to carry food such as seeds, shoots and roots.

descend like this will quickly follow suit and, very soon, all the vultures from kilometres around are converging on the dead animal. The largest birds are in first, ripping open the animal's hide while the smaller ones wait their turn. All the time they are fighting and pecking one another to get at the meal.

Vultures are beautiful birds when soaring in the air. But on the ground – and especially when they are covered in blood and gore after a meal – they are really quite ugly.

The Black Vulture is the largest vulture and one of the ugliest birds in Southern Europe.

Polecat

Polecats spend a great deal of their time walking around with their noses pressed to the ground sniffing for food.

Most active at night, they use their excellent sense of smell – and hearing – to hunt rabbits, mice, hedgehogs, birds, frogs, lizards and a variety of other prey. Polecats are found in many parts of Europe. They are closely related to ferrets, weasels and mink.

Nesting loggerheads

LOGGERHEAD TURTLES spend most of their lives in water, far out at sea. But every year, the females migrate thousands of kilometres to lay their eggs on quiet, sandy beaches. They always wait until the safety of darkness before coming ashore, and it is usually well after midnight before the first ones noisily haul themselves out of the water.

When they have found a suitable spot, they dig a large hole, kicking the sand away with their back flippers. Inside each 'nest', more than a hundred round, white eggs,

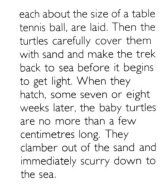

each about the size of a table tennis ball, are laid. Then the turtles carefully cover them with sand and make the trek back to sea before it begins to get light. When they hatch, some seven or eight weeks later, the baby turtles are no more than a few centimetres long. They clamber out of the sand and immediately scurry down to the sea.

SOUTHERN EUROPE
DID YOU KNOW?

Sea horses are fish. However, they are very poor swimmers and have to hang on to seaweed with their tails to avoid being carried along with the ocean currents.

The praying mantis is an insect which other insects prefer to avoid. It hides in the foliage and shoots out its arms – which are as sharp as needles – to impale passing animals. They are then held in a pincer-like grip and slowly eaten alive.

Hoopoes are very beautiful birds – but their nests are extremely smelly – and they have a conspicuous and far-carrying call which sounds like 'pooh-pooh-pooh'.

To avoid being stung, a bee-eater bangs the unfortunate bee on the head several times and then squeezes out the poison by rubbing its stinging end against a branch before eating it.

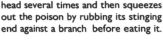

NORTH AMERICA

Grizzly bear
Grizzlies can be very dangerous since they are unable to see very well – and often mistake people for bears. When they feel threatened or annoyed they fight, using their famous 'bear hugs' or strong teeth and claws.

Wolverine
Looking like a cross between a hairy weasel, a dog and a bear, the wolverine is a fearless and very powerful creature. It often fights animals much bigger than itself and has even been seen driving grizzly bears, pumas and packs of wolves away from its food single-handed.

Elf owl
Strange cackling noises can sometimes be heard coming from inside holes in the giant cactus plants of some North American deserts. They are made by elf owls, no bigger than sparrows and among the smallest owls in the world.

ARCTIC OCEAN

ALASKA (USA)

PACIFIC OCEAN

C A N A D A

U N I T E D   S T A T E S

O F   A M E R I C A

MEXICO

NORTH ATLANTIC OCEAN

California sealion
California sealions are probably best known for balancing balls on their noses, clapping with their flippers and blowing circus trumpets. In the wild, they often play together by leaping from the water and diving back headfirst. They are sometimes so playful that they chase and catch their own air bubbles.

Skunk
The skunk is famous for its horrible smell. If an enemy comes too close it waves its tail in the air, stamps its front feet on the ground and struts around in circles. Then it sprays an oily, yellow liquid at the intruder's face. The awful smell can linger for many days after such an 'attack'.

Prairie dog
Prairie dogs are not dogs – but squirrels. They live in enormous 'towns' on the prairies of North America. There are often thousands of them living together in one town, in specially-built burrows which look as if they belong to giant moles.

Burglars in the night

EVERY night, in towns and cities throughout North America, gangs of masked raiders overturn people's dustbins and steal their contents. The raiders, about the size of domestic cats, are raccoons.

Probably the most mischievous animals in the world, they are unmistakable with their 'bandit' masks and bushy, ringed tails.

'Coons', as they are affectionately called, will eat almost anything. Mice, insects, fruit, grains, nuts, berries, frogs, crabs and household scraps are all eagerly taken. They like to live near people and will even beg in small groups by the roadside, where they know passers-by will stop to feed them.

Roadrunner

In the deserts of the southern United States and northern Mexico a very strange bird spends most of its time running backwards and forwards, twisting and turning in and out of the cactus thickets. Clucking and crowing as it goes, the roadrunner can easily outrun a man and often reaches speeds of up to twenty-five kilometres an hour. It can fly – by leaping into the air – but prefers to keep its feet firmly on the ground.

Moose

Moose, or elk as they are sometimes called, are the largest deer in the world. They walk very carefully and quietly through the undergrowth of their woodland homes, trying not to be seen. If they accidentally come across a hunter – and can see no means of escape – they sometimes try to hide behind a tree.

AT one time all the world's continents were joined together. But 100 million years ago this giant landmass – which geologists call Pangaea – began to split. As the North Atlantic opened up, Europe and North America drifted apart by as much as 10 centimetres every year. Today they are separated by several thousand kilometres of ocean – and are still moving away from one another.

According to the history books, America was "discovered" by Christopher Columbus in 1492. But people had been living there for thousands of years before then. The first to arrive

Bald eagle

The bald eagle – which eats fish and lives by rivers and on inland lakes – is the national symbol of the United States. It has a spectacular courtship display, during which the male and female birds lock talons in mid-air and somersault through the air together.

21

MOOSE

HARP SEAL

GREY WHALE

CHIPMUNK

PORCUPINE

SIDEWINDER

PRAIRIE DOG

BEAVER

MONARCH BUTTERFLY

ELF OWL

BALD EAGLE

CALIFORNIA SEALION

ROADRUNNER

MANATEE

Chipmunk

Chipmunks spend nearly all their lives sleeping, eating and collecting food. They can stuff several acorns into their mouths at one time and often hide them under rocks, or logs, or inside their burrows. As winter draws nearer, and the weather gets colder, the chipmunks move underground to sleep. Sometimes they stay in their short burrows for as long as seven months.

Screech owl

Screech owls are fairly small, starling-sized birds. But if they feel threatened they can vigorously defend themselves and their nests. They will attack – and sometimes even kill – animals several times their size.

were probably the Amerindians. They crossed over the land bridge which is now the Bering Strait, between Russia and Alaska, as long as 40,000 years ago.

By 1790 the population of North America – which consists of Canada and the United States – was about five million. Today there are 235 million people living in the United States, and another 30 million in Canada.

The continent is so large that it has been divided into over 60 different states and provinces. Many of these, including Texas, Montana, Alaska, California, Ontario and Newfoundland, are bigger than some European countries.

North America also has great extremes in climate. In Canada's Northwest Territories, high above the Arctic Circle, temperatures have on occasion dropped to minus 60 degrees centigrade. But in Death Valley, California, they can reach as high as plus 60 degrees centigrade.

Grey whale

Twice a year, grey whales swim along the entire length of the west coast of North America. The return trip, between the Arctic Ocean or Alaska and Mexico, is more than 20,000 kilometres. The whales have to undertake these long journeys because all their food is found in the Arctic and they require the warm, shallow waters further south for breeding.

Beware of the spines!

THE body of a porcupine – except its face and underside – is covered in a prickly coat of needle-sharp quills. Usually, these menacing weapons lie flat against the porcupine's body. But if danger threatens they are raised and rattled. Faced with such an alarming sight – and the porcupine's clicking teeth and growling and hissing – most hyenas, lions, martens and other enemies decide to run away.

Many people wrongly believe that the porcupine fires the quills into its enemies. But it actually runs backwards – unable to see where it is going – and, if lucky enough to be on target.

Do mermaids really exist?

THERE are many reports, from years gone by, of sailors seeing mermaids. These strange creatures were supposed to be half woman and half fish. But there is really no such thing. The sailors were actually seeing some animals called manatees. These are really underwater cows, which feed on water grasses and live in the bays, estuaries, rivers and shallow coastal waters of some of the warmer parts of America and Africa.

Manatees are excellent swimmers, able to stay underwater for up to a quarter of an hour, and can reach speeds of 25 kilometres per hour or more. They use their flattened tails as paddles and sometimes 'walk' along the bottom on their flippers.

There are many large towns and cities in North America – including Toronto, Vancouver, Montreal, New York and Los Angeles – but there are also many striking wilderness areas. There are mountains, such as Alaska's Mt. McKinley; great rivers like the Mississippi; deserts such as the Mojave; spectacular waterfalls like Niagara and Yosemite; and many great lakes and forests.

jabs them into the enemy's skin. Many of the quills come off and, although they are not poisonous, often cause quite serious injuries.

Porcupines are related to guinea pigs. There are many different kinds and they are found in many parts of the world. Those living in North and South America have shorter spines than the rest and are able to climb trees; the others live in Europe, Africa and Asia, and prefer to shuffle along the ground.

The passenger pigeon was once the commonest bird on earth. But hunters shot it to extinction in the space of just 50 years. The last survivor – called 'Martha' – died on 1st September 1914, in Cincinnati Zoo, USA.

Harp seal

Harp seals have three favourite breeding grounds: in the White Sea off the coasts of Russia and Scandinavia, in the Greenland Sea north of Jan Mayen island, and in the Newfoundland area of Canada. Their pups are born on the ice, from late February to mid-March.

The first national park in the world – designed to protect areas such as these – was set up in the United States over 100 years ago. Since then, many more have been established on the continent. Areas like Yellowstone, the Everglades and Yosemite are now known worldwide for their scenery and wildlife. They are very important for conservation and protect a wide range of different animals and plants.

The case of the disappearing plants

IN parts of North America, whole plants can sometimes be seen disappearing under the ground. They are being yanked down by pocket gophers, which sometimes nibble at roots entering their underground burrows.

Pocket gophers like to have food available for whenever they feel hungry. So they usually cut it up into small pieces with their sticking-out teeth, then stuff it into special fur-lined cheek pouches with their paws. Then they empty the pouches into their underground larders, to eat whenever they want. It is these pouches, or pockets, which give the gophers their name.

It is possible to hear the wolf's 'lonesome howl' from as far away as sixteen kilometres. Wolves keep in touch with one another by howling – but may also howl for pleasure.

Rattlesnakes can feel vibrations in the ground but, since they cannot 'hear' as we do, are unable to hear the rattling of their own tails.

DICK TWINNEY

24

Among the most interesting animals to be found in North America are the Florida cougar, bald eagle, polar bear, wolf, jaguar, grey whale and the near-extinct black-footed ferret.

Sea otter

Sea otters are excellent swimmers and often dive to the seabed to search for crabs, mussels, fish, snails, sea urchins and other small animals. They eat while lying on their backs on the surface, using their chests as tables. At night, they tie themselves to giant seaweed to avoid drifting out to sea while they are fast asleep.

The animal engineer

RATHER like a giant rat with a flat tail and webbed hind feet, the beaver is always busy building dams, lodges and canals. It has become known as the engineer of the animal world because of all the things it makes out of sticks and mud.

Beavers live in home-made dome-shaped lodges, in streams and small lakes. They work mostly at night, though sometimes have to begin in the afternoon if they are particularly busy. They cut down trees by gnawing the trunks with their teeth. As the trees begin to fall, the beavers scamper out of the way and then carefully return to start cutting them into sections. Each piece is dragged or pushed into the water for building.

Animals hunted for their fur

ANIMALS with beautiful fur coats have been killed by people for centuries. In North America alone, beavers, otters, deer, elk, raccoons, wolves and bears are among the many different creatures that have been trapped and hunted in enormous numbers over the years. Many of these animals have been hunted almost to the point of extinction; some, such as the sea mink, have disappeared altogether. At the same time, each beaver hat or mink coat has meant many hours of pain and terror for the trapped and hunted animals. These days there are also special fur farms where the animals are kept in cages and killed for their fur when they are big enough to make a profit. But many people believe this is cruel. In the wild, the hunting and trapping continues around the world but most of the rarer species, such as tigers, snow leopards and pandas, are protected by law. Nevertheless, poachers still kill the animals illegally and sell them for enormous sums of money on the black market.

The raccoon is very distinctive with its bandit-like face.

NORTH AMERICA

DID YOU KNOW?

Most Texas blind salamanders never see daylight. They live only in deep wells and underground streams in some caves in Texas.

The beautiful monarch, or milkweed, butterfly is the only insect which migrates long distances twice every year. It spends the winter months in California and Mexico but breeds as much as 3,000 kilometres farther north.

Flying squirrels have 'wings' of furry skin between their arms and legs. These enable the animals to glide from one treetop to another, during their search for fruit and nuts.

The jackrabbit's enormous ears are important for detecting the sounds of danger approaching. But they are also used as radiators, to lose heat. The jackrabbit sticks them up in the air if it gets really hot.

The sidewinder is a strange snake that travels sideways. It seems to fly along the ground, as if on a magic carpet, and can travel at up to four kilometres per hour.

CENTRAL AND SOUTH AMERICA

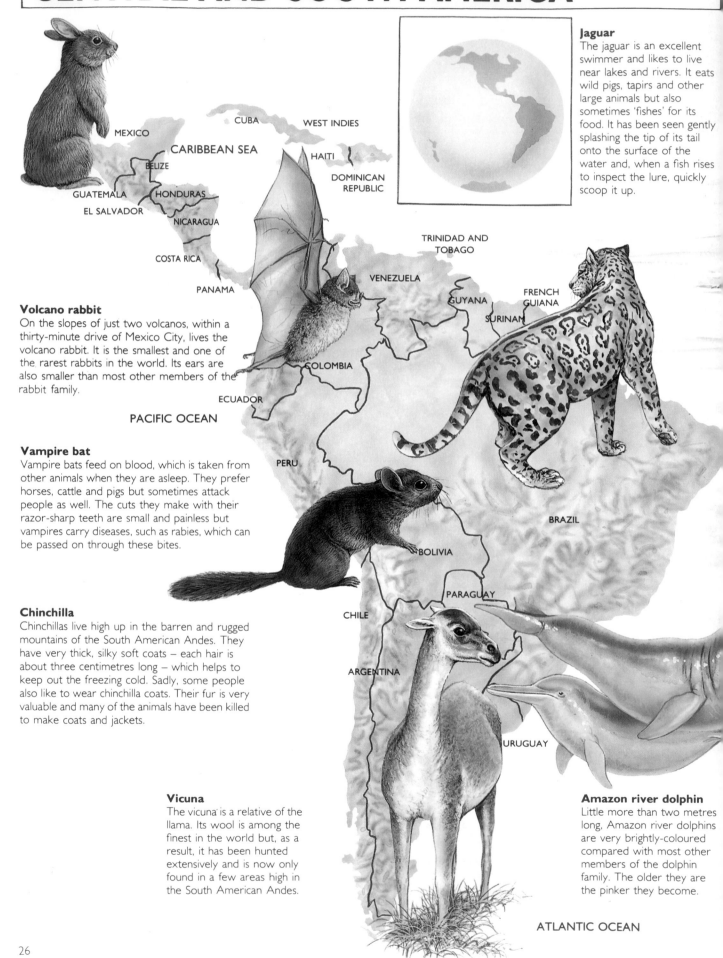

Jaguar
The jaguar is an excellent swimmer and likes to live near lakes and rivers. It eats wild pigs, tapirs and other large animals but also sometimes 'fishes' for its food. It has been seen gently splashing the tip of its tail onto the surface of the water and, when a fish rises to inspect the lure, quickly scoop it up.

MEXICO

CUBA   WEST INDIES

CARIBBEAN SEA

BELIZE

HAITI

GUATEMALA   HONDURAS   DOMINICAN REPUBLIC

EL SALVADOR

NICARAGUA

COSTA RICA

PANAMA

TRINIDAD AND TOBAGO

VENEZUELA

GUYANA   FRENCH GUIANA

SURINAM

COLOMBIA

ECUADOR

PACIFIC OCEAN

PERU

BRAZIL

BOLIVIA

PARAGUAY

CHILE

ARGENTINA

URUGUAY

ATLANTIC OCEAN

Volcano rabbit
On the slopes of just two volcanos, within a thirty-minute drive of Mexico City, lives the volcano rabbit. It is the smallest and one of the rarest rabbits in the world. Its ears are also smaller than most other members of the rabbit family.

Vampire bat
Vampire bats feed on blood, which is taken from other animals when they are asleep. They prefer horses, cattle and pigs but sometimes attack people as well. The cuts they make with their razor-sharp teeth are small and painless but vampires carry diseases, such as rabies, which can be passed on through these bites.

Chinchilla
Chinchillas live high up in the barren and rugged mountains of the South American Andes. They have very thick, silky soft coats – each hair is about three centimetres long – which helps to keep out the freezing cold. Sadly, some people also like to wear chinchilla coats. Their fur is very valuable and many of the animals have been killed to make coats and jackets.

Vicuna
The vicuna is a relative of the llama. Its wool is among the finest in the world but, as a result, it has been hunted extensively and is now only found in a few areas high in the South American Andes.

Amazon river dolphin
Little more than two metres long, Amazon river dolphins are very brightly-coloured compared with most other members of the dolphin family. The older they are the pinker they become.

Condor

Like other members of the vulture family, the condor is an ugly bird on the ground. But in the air it is beautiful and graceful, able to soar effortlessly for hours on end without needing to flap its wings.

Sloth

Sloths spend nearly all their lives hanging upside-down from branches, high up in the jungle trees of Central and tropical South America. They sometimes even remain attached after they have died. They are incredibly slow and inactive animals, moving around at a snail's pace and sleeping for about fifteen hours every day.

Toucan

Toucans are best known for their enormous beaks. These are often very colourful and are extremely strong. The birds use them to frighten off their enemies and to reach fruit which would otherwise be out of reach.

Torrent duck

Torrent ducks live in the fast-flowing rivers of the Andes. These amazing birds spend most of their lives battling against the swirling whitewaters in search of their favourite food – the larvae of stoneflies – which live among the underwater weeds of their river homes.

CENTRAL and South America consist of over 30 nations, from Mexico and Guatemala in the north to Chile in the south. Situated largely in the tropics, the region contains a major share of the world's jungles and is very rich in wildlife. Llamas, monkeys, jaguars, capybaras, giant anteaters and parrots are among the many different creatures to be found there. Unlike Africa, however, there are no really large animals: one of the biggest is the pony-sized tapir.

Central and South America are linked together only by a very narrow strip of land in Panama. About 100 million years ago they were both joined to Africa but they have been moving apart – very slowly – ever since. Today the two

Spider monkey

If you are walking through the jungles of South America and branches start falling on top of you, do not be surprised. They are probably being thrown by spider monkeys, trying to scare you away while they hide in the treetops. But they are not very courageous animals and will slip away and hide if the situation begins to look dangerous.

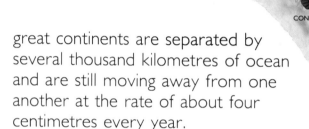

Life in a jungle

WHEN people visit jungles, or tropical rain forests, they rarely see many animals. Looking in from the edge – a river bank or a road, for example – there is often an impenetrable wall of plants blocking any view of the inside.

Those who venture through this wall find a dark and steamy interior. They may hear a few strange sounds, occasional rustlings in the leaves or perhaps the calling of distant birds, but there is often so little sign of life that it can be hard to believe there is any wildlife there at all. Jungles, however, are among the richest habitats in the world and are actually alive with about half all known animal and plant species.

OPOSSUM

4-BANDED ARMADILLO

AMAZON RIVER DOLPHIN

CONDOR

VAMPIRE

HUMMINGBIRD

TOUCAN

SLOTH

TORRENT DUCK

GIANT ANTEATER

VICUNA

great continents are separated by several thousand kilometres of ocean and are still moving away from one another at the rate of about four centimetres every year.

The earliest human inhabitants arrived in the region about 20,000 years ago. By the time Christopher Columbus appeared on the scene in the 15th century, more than 10 million people were living there. Central and South America now contain some of the largest cities in the world, including well-known capitals such as Lima and Mexico City.

There are also some magnificent natural areas. Between the permanent ice and snow on the mountain tops and the steaming jungles along the coast, there are grasslands – known in different countries as llanos, campos and pampas – tundra, deserts and many other different habitats.

These jungle inhabitants are there when people visit, but most are either nocturnal or seldom venture down from the treetops. Others are beautifully camouflaged and almost invisible as they quietly wander around in the dappled light of the forest floor. Most of them will see or hear you first if you walk through 'their' jungle home – so it is often better to sit quietly for a few minutes – and let the animals come to you as they move around undisturbed and unaware of your presence.

Marine iguana

Along the beautiful shores of the Galapagos Islands, many kilometres off the coast of South America, thousands of giant lizards lie out on the rocks to sunbathe. Known as marine iguanas, these two-metre long, completely harmless creatures spend every day warming themselves in the sun. They feed on seaweed and other water plants and are the only lizards in the world which like to live in the sea.

Armadillo

'Armadillo' means 'little armoured one' in Spanish. True to its name, the armadillo is covered in a bony plate of armour, which gives it protection against attacks from enemies and sharp thorns and branches. There are more than twenty different kinds of armadillo, ranging in size from the tiny pink fairy armadillo, measuring just 15 centimetres from head to tail, to the giant armadillo, which is ten times as long. Armadillos are excellent diggers. They can dig a tunnel so rapidly that they vanish almost before their enemies know what is happening.

The Galapagos Islands

ON a map, the Galapagos Islands appear as insignificant little dots in the Pacific Ocean, about a thousand kilometres off the coast of Ecuador. They do not even appear on some world maps. Yet they are unique and, from a naturalist's point of view, one of the most exciting places in the world.

The islands were formed by volcanic eruptions under the sea and are only about one million years old. They were first discovered in 1535, but it wasn't until 300 years later, when they were visited by Charles Darwin, that their importance became apparent.

Disappearing jungles

FROM the highest treetop to the darkest forest floor, the jungles of Central and South America are alive with plants and animals – colourful birds, monkeys, butterflies, beautiful cats and literally hundreds of thousands of others. But, like other jungles around the world, they are being bulldozed and burned to provide more land for farming and ranching and to build roads and towns.

Worldwide, jungles are disappearing so fast that more than half of them have been lost already. Some scientists believe that we are destroying these rich habitats so rapidly that they will be gone completely by the end of the century.

He noticed that many of the animals and plants on the Galapagos resemble species which are found on the South American mainland and yet, at the same time, they are quite different. For example, some are slightly larger or smaller, while others vary a little in colour or have different feeding techniques. Darwin also noticed that a few animals, like the famous giant tortoises, are even different from island to island within the group. It was indeed

here, with these observations, that Darwin began to develop his classic theory of evolution.

In addition to the giant tortoises, other well-known species to be found on the islands include the Galapagos sealion (above), Darwin's finches, marine iguanas, sallylightfoot crabs and Galapagos penguins. They are exciting creatures to see because most of them are extremely tame and seem to show as much interest in human visitors as they do in them!

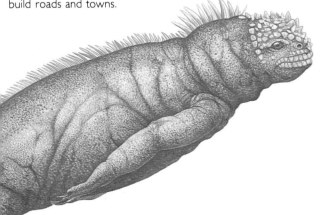

'Lonesome George' is the world's last survivor of the Abingdon saddleback tortoise. He has a shell about a metre long and now lives in captivity at the Charles Darwin Research Station, on Santa Cruz in the Galapagos Islands.

Tamarins in trouble

THE golden lion tamarin is one of the most strikingly-coloured of all the monkeys and apes. It is also one of the rarest. There may be fewer than a hundred of them surviving in the wild, in only two areas of jungle on the coastal mountains of Brazil.

People are cutting down their forest homes and even capture the animals for sale as pets or to zoos.

Sometimes they are eaten by the South American people living nearby.

If nothing is done to protect them from all these hazards, golden lion tamarins could become extinct in the wild by the end of the century.

The world's longest mountain chain and second longest river are both found in South America. The Andes contains no fewer than 50 mountain peaks more than 6,100 metres high and the river Amazon measures an incredible 6,500 kilometres from source to mouth.

Giant guinea-pigs

THE capybara is the largest rodent in the world. It looks like a giant guinea-pig, which is one of its closest relatives.

Capybaras are found near ponds, lakes, streams, rivers and swamps in South America. They normally live together in groups of about ten or twenty – though sometimes as many as a hundred may share the same patch of water during the dry season.

Capybaras spend the hottest part of the day wallowing in mud, or swimming, to keep cool. They are excellent swimmers, using their webbed feet like ducks to paddle along, with just their eyes, ears and noses above the surface. They can even hold their breath underwater for five minutes or more.

HIGH above the ground, in the tops of jungle trees, is a whole world of animals and plants which never come down to earth. Birds, bats, monkeys, snakes, insects and many other creatures eat, sleep and breed among the branches, 40 metres or more above the jungle floor.

Many of these animals have been discovered only quite recently. They have been hidden from view for many years because it is very difficult for people to climb so high. But some scientists

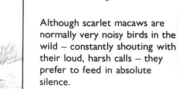

Although scarlet macaws are normally very noisy birds in the wild – constantly shouting with their loud, harsh calls – they prefer to feed in absolute silence.

30

DID YOU KNOW?

Central and South America are home to over half the world's jungles.

If today's rates of destruction continue, there will be virtually no jungles left anywhere in the world by the year 2000. If the jungles disappear, so will half the world's animal and plant species – which live in them.

Giant anteaters walk with their noses close to the ground, always on the look-out for food. They eat up to 30,000 ants and termites every day.

The rare and beautiful quetzal, from Central America, has tail feathers which can grow to over half a metre in length. They drop off at the end of each breeding season and re-grow in time for the following year.

The smallest bird in the world is the bee hummingbird. It weighs nearly 100,000 times less than the ostrich, which is the largest bird in the world.

have built special walkways between the jungle trees and others have been flying over them in hot air balloons. These are the only people who have been able to study the wildlife which lives there.

But they are competing with some real experts at moving around in the tree tops. Various frogs, lizards and snakes, for example, travel from tree to tree by gliding through the air. Some

species swing from branch to branch with their arms while others, including certain monkeys, anteaters, pangolins – and even a kind of porcupine – have special tails which can grip onto branches and make climbing relatively easy. Unlike the scientists, the animals themselves have little or no fear of falling.

Hummingbird
Hummingbirds in flight beat their wings so fast that they are only visible as a blur. They flap up and down almost 80 times every second and enable the birds to hover in mid-air.

When an opossum is threatened by an enemy, it lies limply on its side, with its tongue hanging out of its mouth and its eyes shut or staring into space. It even allows itself to be thrown

around and played with, until the attacker loses interest and moves away to look for livelier prey. This behaviour has given rise to the saying 'playing possum'.

31

AFRICA

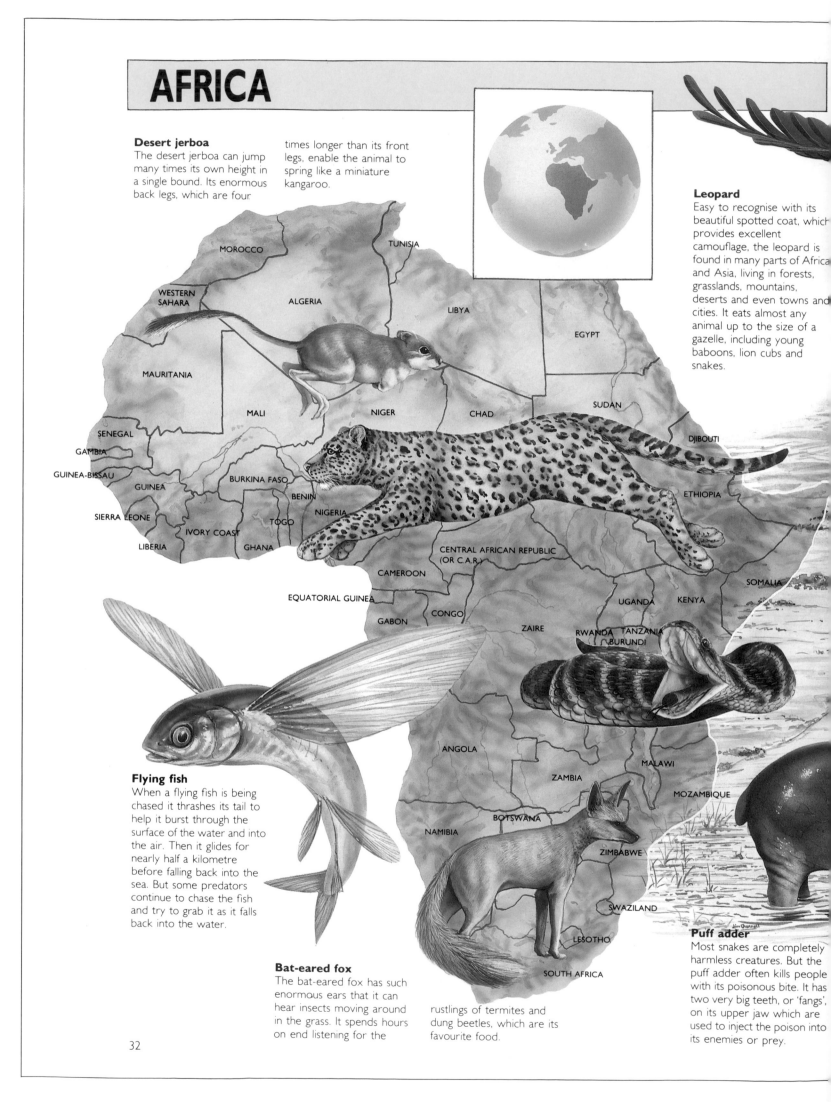

Desert jerboa
The desert jerboa can jump many times its own height in a single bound. Its enormous back legs, which are four times longer than its front legs, enable the animal to spring like a miniature kangaroo.

Leopard
Easy to recognise with its beautiful spotted coat, which provides excellent camouflage, the leopard is found in many parts of Africa and Asia, living in forests, grasslands, mountains, deserts and even towns and cities. It eats almost any animal up to the size of a gazelle, including young baboons, lion cubs and snakes.

Flying fish
When a flying fish is being chased it thrashes its tail to help it burst through the surface of the water and into the air. Then it glides for nearly half a kilometre before falling back into the sea. But some predators continue to chase the fish and try to grab it as it falls back into the water.

Bat-eared fox
The bat-eared fox has such enormous ears that it can hear insects moving around in the grass. It spends hours on end listening for the rustlings of termites and dung beetles, which are its favourite food.

Puff adder
Most snakes are completely harmless creatures. But the puff adder often kills people with its poisonous bite. It has two very big teeth, or 'fangs', on its upper jaw which are used to inject the poison into its enemies or prey.

32

Vulture

Several different vultures are found in Africa. They are all ugly birds on the ground, but in the air they are beautiful and graceful, able to soar effortlessly for hours on end without needing to flap their wings. Vultures usually eat dead animals. Sometimes they eat so much that they cannot take off.

Elephant

The elephant's tusks are really giant teeth which are used for feeding and as weapons. They are very valuable and hundreds of thousands of elephants have been killed in Africa by greedy men who want to sell the tusks to make money.

Ring-tailed lemur

Ring-tailed lemurs are easily recognised by their black-and-white tails, which are always held in the air in the shape of question marks when they are walking or running. They use their tails like flags, to show their friends where they are.

Hippo

The hippo is one of Africa's biggest animals. It comes out at night to eat grass but spends most of its time sleeping and resting in lakes and rivers. Since it weighs as much as three or four tonnes, it does not float to the surface and can easily walk along the bottom.

AFRICA is the second largest continent in the world. It is nearly three times the size of Europe and covers one fifth of all the land on earth.

There are already over 500 million people living in about 50 different countries on the African continent. The population is growing all the time – so in years to come there will be many millions more. Some of these people live in large towns and cities such as Cairo, Lagos, Nairobi, Lusaka, Harare and Kampala. But many live in mud or grass huts, in small villages out in the countryside, where they keep cattle, grow crops and catch fish.

Africa is a very beautiful continent. Although most of it is in the tropics, it has a wide range of different habitats and landscapes. It contains hot

DESERT GERBOA

CAMEL

VULTURE

PUFF ADDER

LEOPARD

LOCUST

SECRETARY BIRD

SPRING HARE

IBIS

STORK

GIRAFFE

EAGLE

GORILLA

ELEPHANT

CROWNED CRANE

HORNBILL

RHINO

LION

CHIMP

HIPPO

FLYING FISH

BAT-EARED FOX

AYE-AYE

RED-BILLED QUELEA

INDRI

HAMMERKOP

AARDVARK

LEMUR

Does ET really exist?

A very strange creature lives in a small area of rain forest on an island off the east coast of Madagascar. Known as the aye-aye, it looks rather like something from outer space. It has rat-like teeth, a bushy, squirrel-like tail, a cat-like body, huge eyes and ears and a long, thin middle finger – just like ET.

But aye-ayes have always lived on earth. They are very rare animals and belong to a group of monkeys known as the lemurs. Their favourite food is grubs, which live under the bark of trees. The aye-aye carefully places one of its ears next to the bark, listening for the slightest sounds of the tiny animals. Then, as soon as it can hear their movements, it quickly gnaws a hole into the tree and pulls out the grubs with its twig-like finger.

Gorilla

Young gorillas spend a great deal of their time playing. They climb trees, slide down tree trunks, wrestle with each other, swing on branches, play chasing games and even irritate the adults in their troop. These playtimes are an important part of growing up. They enable the young gorillas to learn how to climb, find food and do other things like their parents.

Extinction is forever

THE black rhino is one of the rarest animals in Africa. There are only 4,500 of them left on the entire continent.

But less than 20 years ago, there were 65,000 black rhinos. Enormous numbers of them have been killed by poachers – gangs of men with guns – who are after their horns. Rhino horn is more valuable than gold and it is sold to people in the Middle East and Asia for vast sums of money.

Special parks and reserves have been set up to protect the rhinos. Laws were passed several years ago to make rhino poaching illegal. There are even regular patrols of 'rhino security guards' to protect them in the bush. But despite all these efforts rhinos are still being killed. If many more are allowed to die, they may soon disappear from Africa altogether.

- Faro N.P. (Cameroon)
- Kruger N.P. (S. Africa)
- Serengeti N.P. (Kenya/Tanzania)
- Masai Mara N.P. (Kenya)
- Luangua Valley (Zambia)

deserts and steamy jungles, wide expanses of open grassland, Mediterranean woodlands and beautiful tropical coastlines. It also has some of the most beautiful mountains in the world, the highest of which is the 5,895-metre high Mount Kilimanjaro, in Tanzania. Another outstanding natural wonder is the Nile, which is nearly 7,000 kilometres long and one of the longest rivers in the world.

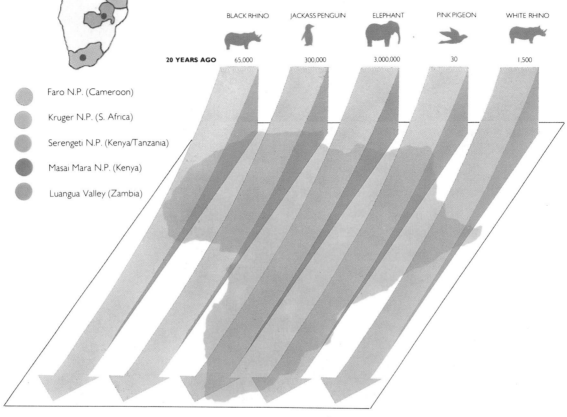

	BLACK RHINO	JACKASS PENGUIN	ELEPHANT	PINK PIGEON	WHITE RHINO
20 YEARS AGO	65,000	300,000	3,000,000	30	1,500
TODAY	4,500	170,000	1,000,000	15	17

Scorpion

Scorpions range in length from less than a centimetre to about 18 centimetres. They all have special stings on the ends of their tails which are used for killing prey and, sometimes, stinging their enemies.

Predators and prey

ALL animals that kill and eat other animals are called 'predators' and their meals are called 'prey'.

Lions eat many different creatures, including wildebeest, zebras, giraffes, buffalos and warthogs. These prey animals have to be able to run very fast if they want to avoid being eaten and are always looking around them in case there are lions nearby. This makes it difficult for the lions to find a meal. They have to creep up on their prey very quietly, or hide in some long grass and then pounce when they are least expected.

The female lions do most of the hunting; the male's mane makes him too easy to see, so his chief role in the pride is to defend it from intruders.

Indri

Indris are very rare animals, found only in the jungles on the slopes of a few volcanos in Madagascar. They make the loudest noise of any animal in Madagascar. It sounds like a mixture between a howling dog and a person crying out in pain – and can be quite spooky.

The wilderness areas of Africa were once teeming with wildlife. There is still plenty to see today – including lions, leopards, baboons, rhinos, ostriches and hippos – but their numbers have declined considerably in recent years. In 1970, for example, there were three million elephants living in many parts of Africa. But so many have been shot for their ivory – or robbed of their homes by growing cities and expanding farmland – that there are now fewer than one million left.

Nowadays, much of Africa's remaining wildlife lives in special national parks set up to protect them. Among these are some of the most spectacular wild places on earth. The Serengeti and Ngorongoro Crater in Tanzania, the Masai Mara in Kenya, Luangwa Valley in Zambia and many others are famous throughout the world. It is the combination of these wilderness areas – and their famous 'big game' – which makes Africa so different from any other continent on earth.

Banded mongoose

The mongoose is famous for being able to kill snakes. Its reactions are so fast that it can dodge each time the snake strikes. As soon as it gets a chance it dives in, grabs the snake and kills it.

Giraffe

THE giraffe is so enormous that its legs alone are sometimes taller than a man. Living on the plains and savannas of Africa, it is a friendly animal and likes the company of other giraffes. But sometimes the males, or bulls, fight one another by banging their heads together or intertwining their necks.

The giraffe's long neck enables it to reach the leaves at the top of acacia trees. Most of its day is spent eating. But it will often go for a stroll, or doze briefly while standing up. Giraffes sometimes lie down at night, but they never sleep properly for more than a few minutes at a time.

No two giraffes have exactly the same pattern – but they all have large spots on their bodies, and smaller ones on their heads and necks. These markings make them surprisingly difficult to see; when they stand in the shade of a tree, their spots blend in with the shadows while their heads are hidden amongst the leaves and branches.

► AFRICAN ◄
BIRDS

LAPPET–FACED VULTURE

FISH EAGLE

GREY-HEADED BUSH SHRIKE

GIANT KINGFISHER

HAMMERKOP

THERE are nearly 9,000 different species of birds in the world. They all have feathers – and all lay eggs – but they come in an incredible variety of different shapes, sizes and colours. Just a look at their beaks gives an idea of this great diversity: the macaw's beak is large and powerful, for cracking open nuts; the woodpecker's is chisel-like for drilling out holes in trees; the eagle's beak is hooked for tearing flesh; and the hummingbird has a long, thin beak for sucking nectar out of flowers.

Africa is particularly rich in birds. Some African countries, such as Kenya, are fortunate in having more than 1,000 different species. Among them are hornbills, ibises, vultures, hammerkops, crowned cranes and yellow-billed storks.

RED–BILLED QUELEA

The largest bird on earth – the ostrich – also lives in Africa. It is half a metre taller than an average- sized man and its eggs are so enormous each one is said to be able to make over 70 omelettes.

RED-BILLED HORNBILL

There is no truth in the popular belief that ostriches bury their heads in the sand. They often feed with their heads hidden down among the vegetation – but regularly raise them to scan the landscape for lions and other dangerous animals. Ostriches are unable to fly but, if danger is approaching, will run away across the plains at speeds of up to 50 kilometres per hour.

GREY PARROT

CROWNED CRANE

One of the strangest inhabitants of the African plains is the secretary bird. It has long, stork-like legs, with black 'plus- fours', and some very long feathers on the back of its head. The bird gets its name from these feathers, which look like the pen quills people used to write with in the olden days. But the secretary bird is not a stork – it actually belongs to the same group of birds as the hawks and eagles. It spends its days walking along the ground in search of insects, small rodents and snakes. It kills large snakes by stamping on them.

SECRETARY BIRD

GLOSSY IBIS

PIN-TAILED WHYDAH

The commonest bird in Africa – indeed, in the whole world – is the red-billed quelea. A small, sparrow-like bird with a pinky-red bill, it can sometimes be seen in flocks of up to a million. There are thought to be at least twice as many red-billed queleas in the world as there are people.

SADDLEBILL

OSTRICH

HELMETED GUINEA-FOWL

GOLDEN-TAILED AFRICAN WOODPECKER

CATTLE EGRET

Hyena

At night, in many parts of Africa, it is common to hear strange giggles, yells and growls, weird howling screams and blood-curdling laughter. All these noises are made by the spotted, or laughing, hyena, which comes out to eat after dark.

SAHARA DESERT

The Sahara Desert is the largest desert in the world. It covers an area about the size of the United States of America — and is still growing.

Aardvark

The aardvark is a very strange-looking animal. It has a long, sticky, worm-shaped tongue for licking up ants and termites.

How clever are chimpanzees?

CHIMPANZEES are very intelligent animals. They live in the jungles and grasslands of Africa and are very similar and closely-related to people. They often hold hands when they are together; they kiss when they meet; and can even smile, or look worried when something is troubling them. Unlike most other monkeys and apes, they are able to use tools.

Living in the desert

THE camel is perfectly adapted to living in the desert. It has bushy eyebrows and plenty of eyelashes to keep out the desert sand; and it even has a tough mouth which is unharmed by the sharp thorns of desert plants.

Camels' humps are also very important. They act as storage containers — but not to store water, as many people wrongly believe. They are full of fat, which nourishes the camels when food is scarce.

Like all desert animals, the camel has to be able to survive on small and irregular supplies of water.

For example, they lower sticks into ants' nests, wait for the ants to crawl up, then sweep them into their mouths before they have time to bite. Chimps have even been known to use leaves as sponges by dipping them in water and then washing all over.

AFRICA
DID YOU KNOW?

The longest earthworm in the world comes from South Africa. It can reach a length of seven metres and is so large that it can be heard from above ground as it moves through its tunnels.

The ostrich is the largest living bird in the world. It is 97,000 times heavier than the bee hummingbird, which is the smallest bird in the world.

The highly venomous gaboon viper of tropical Africa has the longest fangs in the world, measuring up to five centimetres long.

The longest neck in the world belongs to the giraffe, which is also the tallest land animal. It is up to four times as tall as a man from the ground to the tips of its horns.

The noisiest monkey in the world is the howler monkey. Its cries and howls can be heard up to five kilometres away.

Normally, it gets all the moisture it needs from desert plants and can survive for up to 10 months without drinking any water at all. But when it is really thirsty it can drink as much as 136 litres of water – that's about 500 full glasses – in just 10 minutes.

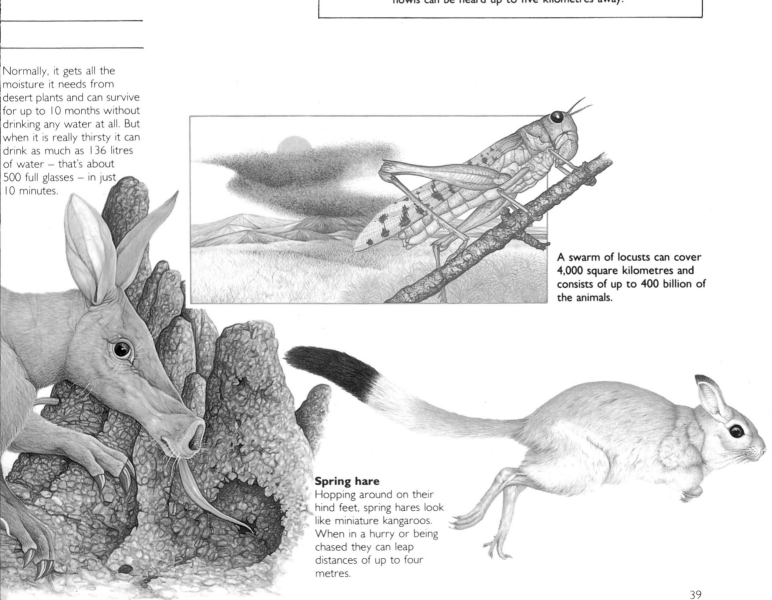

A swarm of locusts can cover 4,000 square kilometres and consists of up to 400 billion of the animals.

Spring hare
Hopping around on their hind feet, spring hares look like miniature kangaroos. When in a hurry or being chased they can leap distances of up to four metres.

MIDDLE EAST AND ASIA

ASIA is the largest of all the continents. Stretching almost halfway across the world, from Saudi Arabia to New Guinea, it contains over 40 different countries. Nearly 8,000 kilometres long and over 6,000 kilometres from the frozen north to the tropical south, the land and its people are probably more varied than on any other continent.

In terms of size, Asia contains both the largest and some of the smallest nations in the world. At one extreme is the USSR – which covers an area considerably bigger than Canada and the United States combined – while at the other

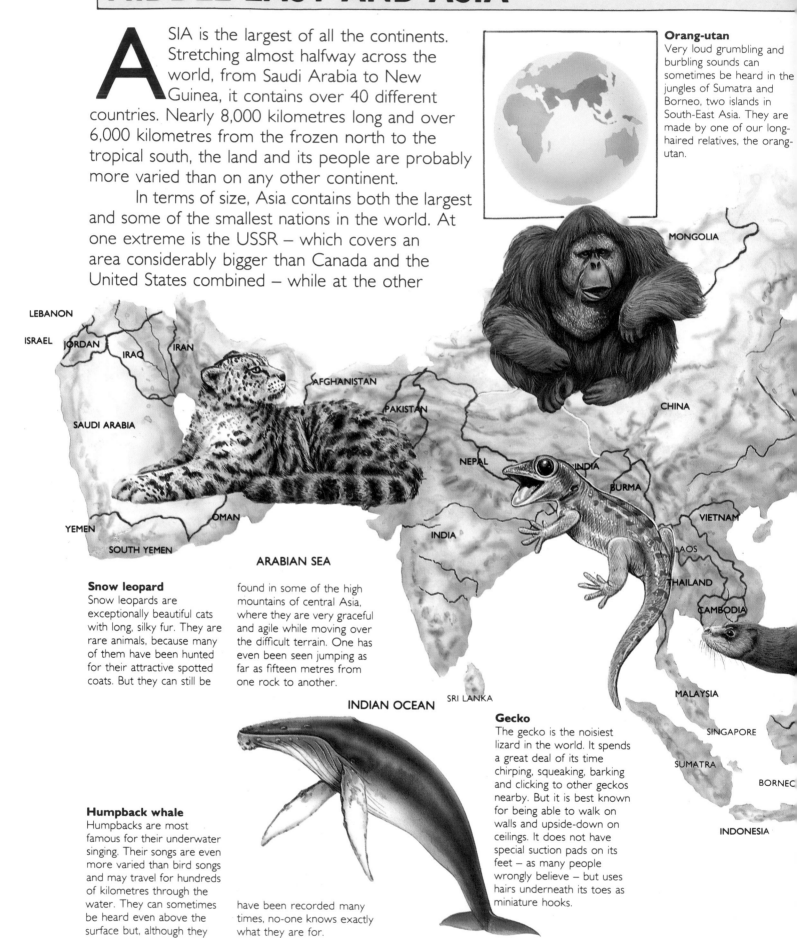

Orang-utan
Very loud grumbling and burbling sounds can sometimes be heard in the jungles of Sumatra and Borneo, two islands in South-East Asia. They are made by one of our long-haired relatives, the orang-utan.

Snow leopard
Snow leopards are exceptionally beautiful cats with long, silky fur. They are rare animals, because many of them have been hunted for their attractive spotted coats. But they can still be found in some of the high mountains of central Asia, where they are very graceful and agile while moving over the difficult terrain. One has even been seen jumping as far as fifteen metres from one rock to another.

Humpback whale
Humpbacks are most famous for their underwater singing. Their songs are even more varied than bird songs and may travel for hundreds of kilometres through the water. They can sometimes be heard even above the surface but, although they have been recorded many times, no-one knows exactly what they are for.

Gecko
The gecko is the noisiest lizard in the world. It spends a great deal of its time chirping, squeaking, barking and clicking to other geckos nearby. But it is best known for being able to walk on walls and upside-down on ceilings. It does not have special suction pads on its feet – as many people wrongly believe – but uses hairs underneath its toes as miniature hooks.

Scorpionfish
The highly poisonous scorpionfish has many different names, including zebrafish, lionfish, dragonfish, firefish, devilfish, turkeyfish and featherfish. It injects the poison into its enemies through long, sharp spines.

Tiger
Tigers are the largest members of the cat family. Only a century ago, there were a hundred thousand of them living all over Asia. But today there are only a few thousand left. All the others have been shot, trapped or poisoned by people. Nowadays there are special laws to protect them – and tiger reserves where they can live in safety – but their numbers have only just started to increase once again.

NORTH KOREA

JAPAN

SOUTH KOREA

PHILIPPINES

Komodo dragon
The Komodo dragon of Indonesia is easily the biggest lizard in the world. Measuring three metres long, it eats wild pigs and deer and has been known to attack and kill people.

Otter civet
In parts of south-east Asia, thirsty birds and other small animals visiting a stream or swamp to drink have to be very careful. Quietly hiding in the water, with only the tip of its nose showing above the surface, may be an otter civet waiting to pounce.

there are several tiny tropical island nations. One of these is the Maldives, in the Indian Ocean, which covers an area of less than 300 square kilometres.

Two out of every three people – nearly 3,000 million – live in Asia. Southern Asia is more tightly packed with people than anywhere else in the world. The overall record-holder is Macau, on the

41

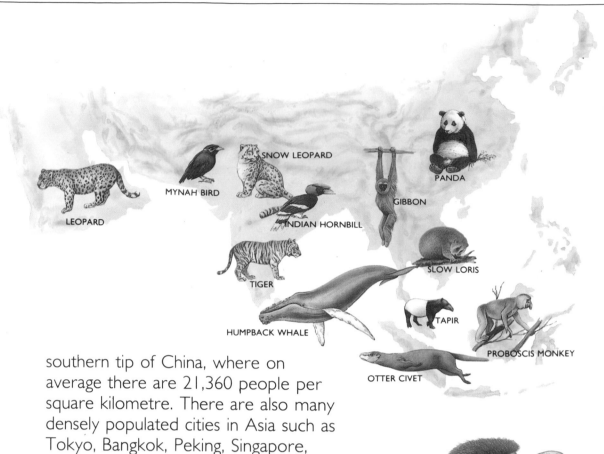

SNOW LEOPARD

MYNAH BIRD

LEOPARD

PANDA

GIBBON

INDIAN HORNBILL

TIGER

SLOW LORIS

HUMPBACK WHALE

TAPIR

PROBOSCIS MONKEY

OTTER CIVET

Hearing you loud and clear

THE proboscis monkey is the elephant of the monkeys and apes. It has an enormous nose – sometimes over seven centimetres long – which hangs down over its mouth and almost touches its chin. This strange contraption is used as a loudspeaker for the animal's warning honk, which sounds rather like a noisy goose and can be heard some distance away.

Only the males have long noses, which swell or become red when they get angry or excited, in much the same way as people blush when they are embarrassed. The females have smaller noses and make milder calls, while the young animals have turned-up noses.

southern tip of China, where on average there are 21,360 people per square kilometre. There are also many densely populated cities in Asia such as Tokyo, Bangkok, Peking, Singapore, Bombay and Manila.

But in some parts of the continent people are few and far between. Mongolia, for example, has a population density of only about one person per square kilometre. Places like the Gobi desert, in Mongolia, are too wild and inhospitable for most people. Mountains can also be difficult places to live and Asia – which contains the 25 highest peaks in the world – is full of them. The most famous – and tallest – of these is Mount Everest. An incredible 8.85 kilometres high, it was first climbed on May 29, 1953.

It is in wilderness areas such as these that rare animals like the snow leopard and Przewalski's horse – perhaps even the so-called yeti – can sometimes be found. Asia has a magnificent collection of wildlife: tigers, elephants,

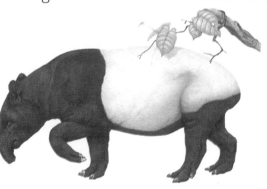

Malayan tapir

Tapirs spend a great deal of their time trying to keep cool. They are excellent swimmers and often lounge around in water during the heat of the day. Baby tapirs look quite different to their striking black-and-white parents. They have brown coats, dappled with white spots and stripes.

Mimicry

ASIA is the home of the mynahs, attractive birds which belong to the starling family and are internationally famous for being able to mimic other animal sounds. Some mynahs can even imitate human voices and sounds as diverse as a closing door or a telephone.

Many other birds can imitate the sounds that they hear. Budgerigars can be taught to say 'hello'; some parrots can learn quite long sentences in a range of different languages from Swahili to Greek; and male marsh warblers each imitate, on average, 76 other species. Many birds even have different 'dialects' – which vary depending on where they live – just as people in New York sound different from people in Texas.

Jungle cat

Although they can be seen wandering around in broad daylight, jungle cats are most active at night. They have excellent eyesight and are also able to find their way in the dark using their whiskers. They can feel trees and other obstacles in the jungle when their whiskers brush against them.

Endangered species

THERE may be as many as ten million different kinds of animals and plants living in the world today. But many of them – perhaps hundreds of thousands – are extremely rare. There is only one surviving dusky seaside sparrow, for example, only a dozen northern white rhinos and fewer than 500 Indus dolphins. These and other creatures like them are 'endangered species'. Animals and plants which have disappeared altogether are 'extinct' – like the dodo, great auk, pink pigeon, Atlas bear, Bali tiger and the strange-looking quagga. It is believed that about 1,000 species become extinct around the world every year.

There are many different reasons why this happens. Most extinctions are caused by people. We hunt and trap animals, for example, and we destroy their homes – by chopping down jungles, or by draining swamps and marshes.

The giant panda is perhaps the most famous endangered species in the world. Once a very common and widespread animal in China, it is now only found in a few remote bamboo forests in the south-west of the country. There are thought to be between 400 and 1,000 survivors left.

Snakes in the house!

SNAKES are particularly common animals in the crowded cities of India, Vietnam, Thailand and other parts of Asia. Russell's and saw-scaled vipers, cobras, copperheads, kraits, rat snakes and many others are often found in people's houses and other city buildings. They hide in the attics, behind cupboards, under beds and in any other suitable nooks and crannies. Some city snakes are very dangerous. They bite and sometimes kill hundreds, or even thousands, of people every year. But most are fairly small and harmless, preferring to mind their own business than attack their human neighbours.

orang-utans, komodo dragons, rhinoceroses, giant pandas and many others. But, sadly, as the human population increases in the region, more and more of these creatures are declining in numbers and becoming endangered.

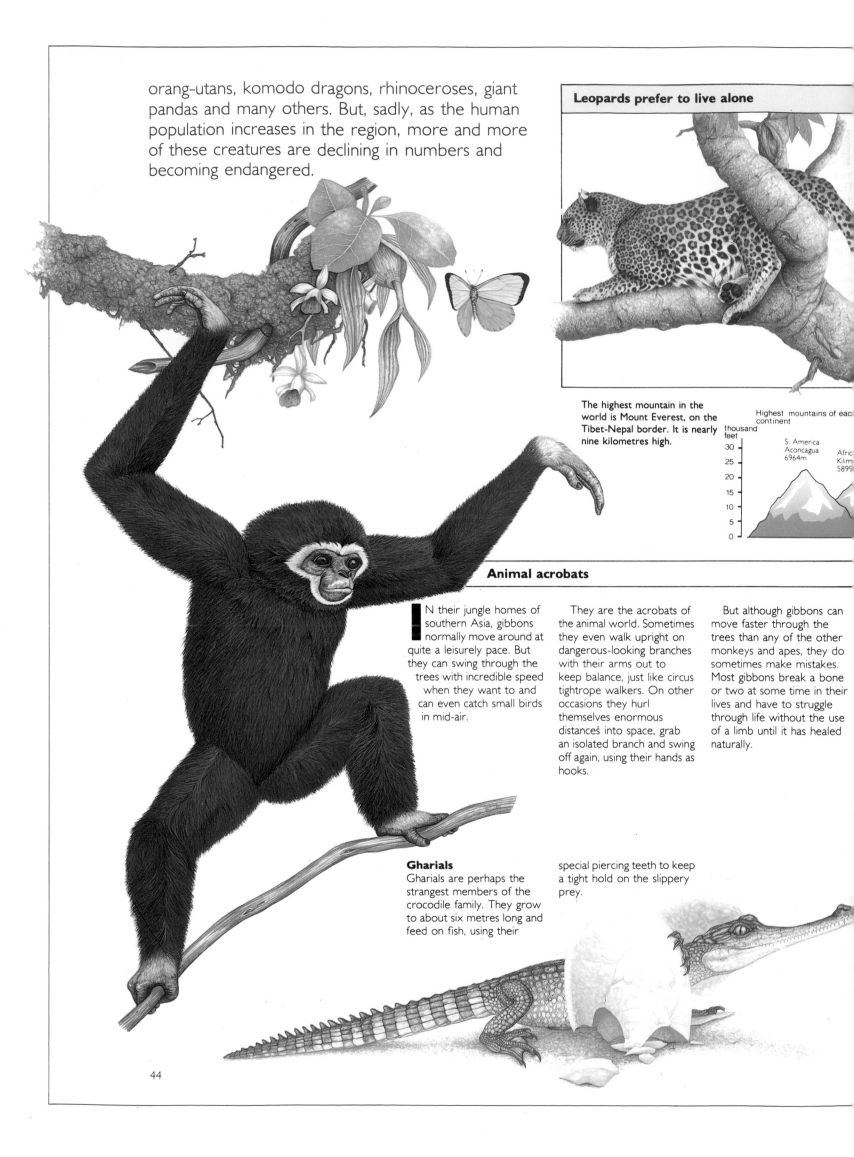

The highest mountain in the world is Mount Everest, on the Tibet-Nepal border. It is nearly nine kilometres high.

Highest mountains of each continent

thousand feet
30
25
20
15
10
5
0

S. America
Aconcagua
6964m

Afric
Kilim
5899

Animal acrobats

IN their jungle homes of southern Asia, gibbons normally move around at quite a leisurely pace. But they can swing through the trees with incredible speed when they want to and can even catch small birds in mid-air.

They are the acrobats of the animal world. Sometimes they even walk upright on dangerous-looking branches with their arms out to keep balance, just like circus tightrope walkers. On other occasions they hurl themselves enormous distances into space, grab an isolated branch and swing off again, using their hands as hooks.

But although gibbons can move faster through the trees than any of the other monkeys and apes, they do sometimes make mistakes. Most gibbons break a bone or two at some time in their lives and have to struggle through life without the use of a limb until it has healed naturally.

Gharials
Gharials are perhaps the strangest members of the crocodile family. They grow to about six metres long and feed on fish, using their

special piercing teeth to keep a tight hold on the slippery prey.

EXCEPT at mating time, leopards usually prefer to avoid meeting other leopards. They let one another know they are around by roaring – not like a lion, but with a roar that sounds more like someone sawing wood. They hunt on their own, travelling in a slow, silent walk as much as 25 kilometres in a single night.

Although the leopard is a night animal, it can often be seen sunning itself in trees and on rocks. Easy to recognise with its beautiful spotted coat, which provides excellent camouflage, it is found in many parts of Africa and Asia, living in forests, grasslands, mountains, deserts and even towns and cities.

MIDDLE EAST AND ASIA

DID YOU KNOW?

The Javan rhinoceros is one of the rarest of the world's rhinoceroses. There are fewer than fifty survivors, living in West Java, Indonesia.

The world's smallest bat is the Kitti's hog-nosed bat – otherwise known as the bumblebee bat – which lives in a small number of caves in Thailand and is smaller than an adult's thumb.

The Ganges dolphin, which lives in the muddy Ganges river of India, is blind. It uses sonar and the sense of touch to find its way around and to locate fish and crabs.

The Asiatic lion is so rare that it can only be found in one place. Fewer than 200 of the animals live in the Gir Forest, India, and nowhere else in the world.

The great Indian hornbill nests in holes in trees. The male blocks the entrance with mud, trapping the female inside to make sure that she incubates the eggs properly.

Europe
Mont Blanc
4810m

Asia
Everest
8854m

Australasia
Cook
3766m

N. America
McKinley
6198m

Antarctica
Vinson Massip
5142m

m
10
9
8
7
6
5
4
3
2
1
0

The highest living wild mammal in the world is probably the yak. It lives in Tibet and the Szechwanese Alps, China, where it occasionally climbs to over 6,000 metres.

Slow loris

Slow lorises really are slow. But very few people have been lucky enough to see one in the wild. They are secretive animals which only come out at night and spend most of their time hidden from sight in the trees. They live in the jungles and bamboo forests of Asia.

AUSTRALASIA

Dingo
The dingo is a very close relative of the domestic dog. It probably arrived in Australia with people, about 8,000 years ago, but has gradually become wild again. Dingoes hunt mostly at night (either alone or in family groups) for rabbits, rats, lizards and birds. They also sometimes eat small kangaroos. Over the years, hundreds of thousands of dingoes have been killed unnecessarily by sheep farmers, in the mistaken belief that they prey regularly on their animals.

Kangaroo
Some kangaroos are able to cover more than eight metres in a single hop. Using their long hind legs to jump and their enormous tails to keep balance in mid-air, they can sometimes reach speeds of up to 50 kilometres per hour.

Spiny anteater
When they are frightened, spiny anteaters can burrow into the ground so fast that looks as if they are sinking. But if the ground is too hard to dig they curl up into a spiky ball, or dive into a nearby hiding place with only the spines on their backs still visible.

INDIAN OCEAN

A U S T R A L I A

AUSTRALASIA is a vast collection of lands spread across the South Pacific Ocean. The region includes Australia, Papua New Guinea, New Zealand and as many as 30,000 far-flung islands – many of which are only tiny rocks barely visible above the waves – stretching over thousands and thousands of kilometres.

Australia itself has a population of only sixteen million people – though even this is considerably more than all the other countries and islands put together – and is so large that it is the only country in the world also regarded as a continent.

Barn owl
Barn owls hunt at night, with the help of their remarkable hearing and eyesight. A cloudy, moonless night probably appears no darker to one of these birds than a rather dim, overcast day does to us.

Wombat
Wombats look rather like small bears, but their closest relative is the koala. Found in south-eastern Australia, Tasmania and on some nearby islands, they live mostly in eucalyptus forests. Unlike koalas, however, they spend all their time on the ground.

46

Duck-billed platypus
The duck-billed platypus is one of the strangest animals in the world. It has webbed feet and a 'beak' like a duck; and it even lays eggs. But it also spends a lot of time underwater, and has fur and a flat tail like a beaver.

Kookaburra
The kookaburra, or laughing jackass, is famous for its noisy, laugh-like call. Largest of all kingfishers, it prefers wooded country and gardens to rivers and lakes and eats mostly mice, insects and small snakes, instead of fish.

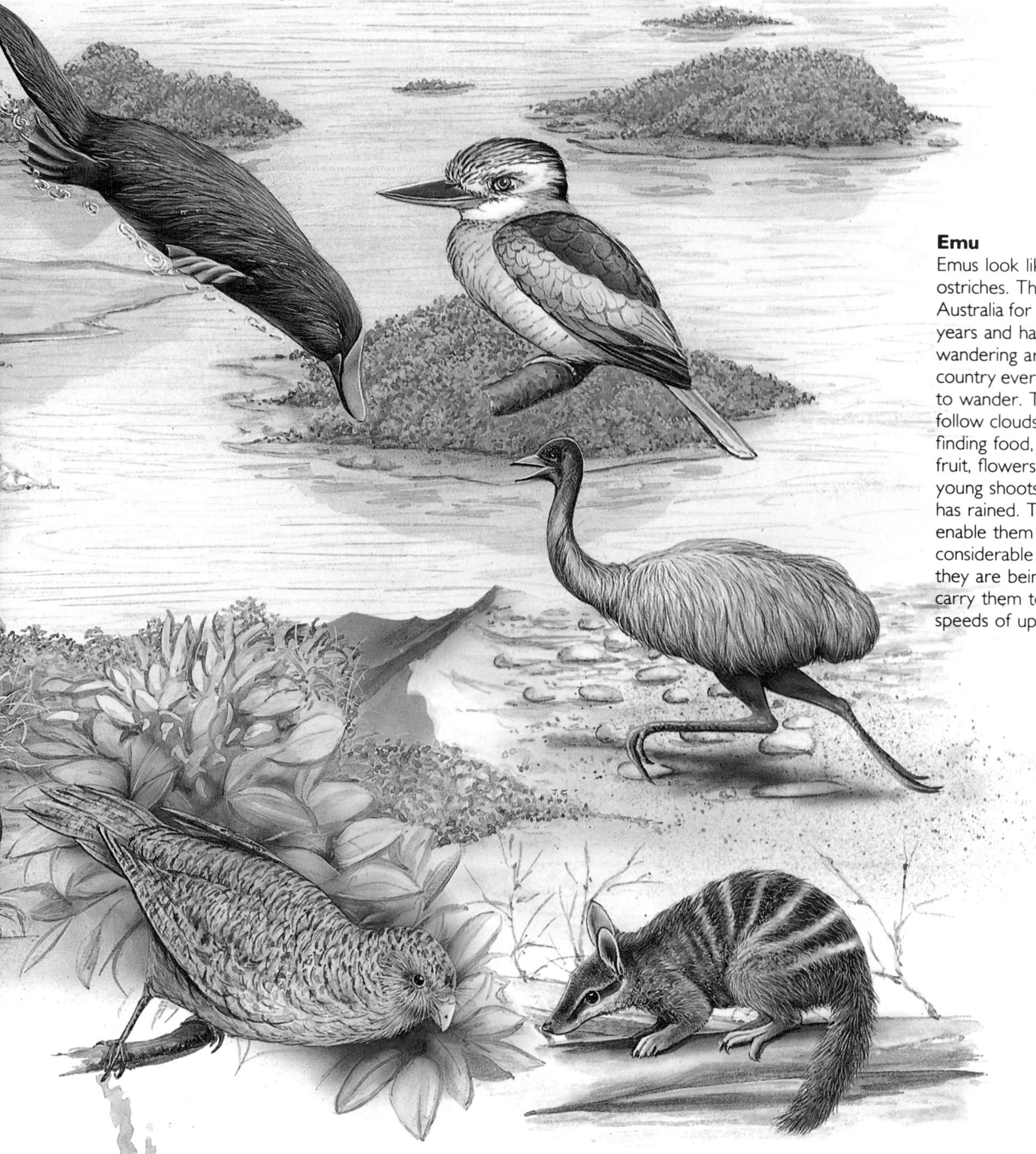

Emu
Emus look like small shaggy ostriches. They have lived in Australia for about 80 million years and have been wandering around the country ever since. Emus like to wander. They often follow clouds, in the hope of finding food, such as seeds, fruit, flowers, insects and young shoots, wherever it has rained. Their long legs enable them to walk considerable distances and, if they are being chased, can carry them to safety at speeds of up to 48km/hour.

NEW ZEALAND

Kakapo
The kakapo is a very rare parrot, which lives in only two remote areas of New Zealand. But it is unlike other parrots because it cannot fly and only comes out at night.

It also makes an extraordinary booming call, similar to the sound made by blowing across the top of an empty bottle.

Numbat
Numbats are always busy searching for food. They eat mostly termites – often several thousand in a day – which are lapped up with their long, thin tongues. At night, they sleep in a hole in the ground or a hollow log.

47

ANTEATER

DUCK-BILLED PLATYPUS

FRILLED LIZARD

SHARK

BARN OWL

FROGMOUTH

EMU

DINGO

WOMBAT

RED KANGAROO

KIWI

KOALA BEAR

KAKAPO

TASMANIAN TIGER

Is it really extinct?

TASMANIAN tigers once used to be quite common animals, but so many have been killed by hunters and by disease that they are now thought by many people to be extinct. As their name suggests, they used to live in Tasmania. The last known survivor died there in 1936.

Since then, many people have searched all over Tasmania for the animals, but with no success. Some people do still claim that they exist, but most scientists think it is very unlikely.

The Tasmanian tiger is not really a tiger. Although it has tiger-like stripes, it is actually a relative of the kangaroo. It even has a pouch, in which to carry around its young for the first few months of their lives.

The first people to live there were the Aborigines, who probably arrived from across the sea in south-east Asia about 40,000 years ago. When Europeans began to settle in Australia, in the late eighteenth century, there were about 300,000 Aborigines. But these days there are barely 135,000 left.

Papua New Guinea is the next largest country in the region. It consists of the eastern half of the island of New Guinea (the remainder belongs to Indonesia) and some nearby islands.

Dangerous animals

MANY different animals (and plants) are capable of killing people. Sharks, snakes, crocodiles, lions, scorpionfish, grizzly bears, elephants, jellyfish, tarantulas, tigers and even frogs have all been responsible for many human deaths over the years.

Some snakes are capable of killing a person within minutes of delivering their deadly bites; there are tales of tigers killing hundreds of people single-handed over periods of several years; and an electric eel can kill a fully-grown man standing several metres away.

Australia has more potentially dangerous animals than most countries. There have been more shark attacks around the

Next in size is New Zealand, which consists of two large islands (and many smaller ones) and has only been inhabited by people for about 1,000 years.

Australasia is so large that it contains an enormous range of different habitats. These include tropical islands, great rivers such as the Darling, 2,740 kilometres long, mountains like Mt. Cook and Mt. Kosciusko, vast deserts and cities such as Sydney, Aukland and Canberra.

It also contains some of the greatest natural wonders to be seen anywhere in the world. Perhaps the most famous of these is the Great Barrier Reef, an incredible maze of islands and reefs which teems with wildlife – fish, birds, crabs, sea urchins and many others – and stretches for 2,000 kilometres along the Queensland coast.

Australian termite nests – or 'castles' – can be over six metres high. They often contain several tonnes of sand, which the termites have built up, grain by grain, over the centuries.

Australian coasts than anywhere else in the world and, on the land, there is a sizeable collection of poisonous spiders, scorpions, snakes and other creatures. The world's most dangerous spider – the Sydney funnelweb – even lives in people's houses, right in the middle of Sydney.

But most animals prefer to avoid people whenever they can and rarely attack unless they are teased, frightened or injured. Most snakes, for example, will try to hide if they hear people coming – and will only bite if they are trodden on – even if their 'attacker' does it by mistake. Even the most dangerous sharks – such as the hammerhead or great white – often swim right past swimmers with barely a second glance.

In fact, many more animals are killed or injured by people than the other way around. Millions of animals are killed every year for their fur or other trophies, for food, for sport and, indirectly, through pollution, habitat destruction and many other human activities.

Shark

The shark is probably the most feared animal in the world. With its streamlined body, needle-sharp teeth, glaring eyes and a nose that can smell food from many kilometres away, it has a terrible reputation. But not all sharks are dangerous. Some are barely fifteen centimetres long and would be incapable of causing much harm. Two of the world's biggest – the fifteen-metre long whale shark and the ten-metre long basking shark – both eat tiny animals called plankton and are completely harmless.

Wild Australian dingos are close relatives of the domestic dog. They used to be trained as 'blankets' and taught to sleep in a huddle with their owners, to provide protection from the cold.

For naturalists, Australasia is a particularly interesting region as it has many unique animals and plants which are found nowhere else in the world. There are kangaroos, wallabies, dingos, Tasmanian tigers, duck-billed platypuses, spiny anteaters, bandicoots, kookaburras, emus, kiwis, budgerigars, cockatoos and many others. There is even a giant earthworm which can grow to over three metres long when fully extended!

KANGAROOS are famous for keeping their young in a special pouch on the mother's tummy. They usually have one tiny baby, called a joey. As soon as it is born, the joey crawls into the safety of the pouch. It stays there for several months, growing and developing, before venturing into the outside world. At first, it is very nervous and, if danger threatens, will run back to its mother and dive into her pouch headfirst. But it gradually gets more daring and begins to wander further and further afield until it is able to look after itself.

Many other animals have pouches. They are called marsupials. There are 92 different marsupials in North, Central and South America; 53 in New Guinea; and about 120 in Australia. Some of the better-known Australian marsupials are Tasmanian devils, bandicoots, possums, wallabies, koalas and wombats.

The frogmouth is a bird — so-called because it has an enormous, gaping mouth.

Koala
The koala looks just like a bear. But it is actually related to kangaroos — and female koalas have pouches on their bellies to prove it. They live in gum trees in south-eastern Australia.

Kiwi

Living in the forests and scrublands of New Zealand is a very strange bird. Known as the kiwi, it cannot fly and only comes out at night. It has very small eyes but can see well enough to run at high speed through the dense undergrowth. The kiwi eats a variety of food, including worms, spiders, beetles and seeds.

The kiwi is the national bird of New Zealand.

Australian frilled lizard

Most lizards run away or hide when they are frightened or under attack. But the Australian frilled lizard stands firm and tries to scare its enemies away. It opens out a gigantic flap of loose skin behind its head and inflates its body. This makes it look much bigger — and much more dangerous — than it actually is.

The scales on a scrawled file fish are so rough that the unfortunate animal was once used as sandpaper.

AUSTRALASIA

DID YOU KNOW?

The largest structure ever built by living creatures is the 2028 kilometre long Great Barrier Reef, off Queensland, Australia. It consists of countless millions of dead and dying stony corals, piled on top of one another, and has taken hundreds of millions of years to build.

The weedy sea dragon is a seahorse that disguises itself as a piece of floating seaweed. It lives around the Australian coast.

Megapodes are birds which build enormous nests on the ground from piles of rotting vegetation. These compost heaps generate the heat which is necessary to incubate the eggs.

THE POLES

LAPLAND BUNTING

POLAR BEAR

ARCTIC CIRCLE

ARCTIC TERN

WALRUS

MUSK OX

REINDEER

SNOWSHOE HARE

KILLER WHALE

ALBATROSS

WEDDELL SEAL

ANTARCTICA

KRILL

SHEATHBILL

ELEPHANT SEAL

EMPEROR PENGUIN

BLUE WHALE

NARWHAL

Emperor penguin
The emperor penguin has to put up with colder weather than any other bird in the world. At its breeding grounds in the Antarctic, temperatures drop to minus

Reindeer
Reindeer live on the tundra and in the forests of the Arctic. They have thick, woolly coats to protect them against the cold and broad hooves, which act like snowshoes in deep snow.

Arctic fox
Arctic foxes live in the colder regions of northern Europe and North America. Their dense woolly coats help them to survive temperatures as low as minus 80 degrees centigrade. White in winter and brown in summer, they also provide perfect camouflage against the changing colours of the Arctic landscape.

Walrus

Walrus tusks are enormous teeth. They never stop growing and, unless they are broken off in an accident, can be a metre or more in length. The tusks have many uses, including breaking through ice, fighting and even for hanging onto the ice to keep their owners' heads above water while they sleep.

Killer whale

Killer whales eat porpoises, dolphins, seabirds, squid, fish, seals and even other whales. But they do not really deserve their 'killer' name. They never kill for fun and only very rarely attack people.

Albatross

Albatrosses have enormous wings, enabling them to glide for hour after hour over the southern seas. The largest of all these beautiful and graceful birds is the wandering albatross, which has an incredible wingspan of three and a half metres.

20 degrees centigrade. Strong winds blow up to 75 kilometres an hour and the unfortunate bird sometimes has to sit for days on end covered in snow.

Musk ox

The longest hair of any animal in the world belongs to the musk ox. Sometimes its furry tufts can be nearly a metre in length. The musk ox's long, thick coat is important to keep it warm and to keep off the mosquitos which are so common on the Arctic tundra. It also helps to provide some protection from predators.

THE Arctic and the Antarctic – known together as the poles – are among the most beautiful wild places on earth. Their unique combination of mountains, pure white snow, beautiful seascapes, clear blue skies and spectacular ice formations is unforgettable.

But both are very cold and inhospitable places to live. Their year is divided into one long day and one long night. During the long, dark winter it never gets light; and during the short summer it never gets dark.

But the two poles – as far apart as it is possible to get – are very different. The Arctic is mostly frozen ocean surrounded by land; the Antarctic is land – covering an area the size of the whole of western Europe – surrounded by ocean.

Sheathbill

Sheathbills look rather like doves but behave more like crows. They eat almost anything they can find. As well as scraps left behind by Antarctic explorers and scientists, they often hunt along rocky shorelines for small animals or bits of fish. But most of all they rely on penguins for their food. They eat penguin eggs, steal their meals and even eat their droppings.

Narwhal

Narwhals are relatives of the whales and dolphins. They only have two teeth and, in the male. one of these grows so big that it sticks out through his upper lip and forms a spiralling tusk. Such tusks have been known to grow to three metres long. No one really knows what the tusks are for, though narwhals have been seen using them like swords, fencing together on the ocean surface.

Compared with other parts of the world, there are relatively few species of animals and plants living in either region. But those which can survive the difficult climate and terrain often occur in enormous numbers. During the summer, in the Antarctic, there are large numbers of seals and literally millions of penguins, skuas, albatrosses and other birds. Most of them live around the coast, since the Antarctic is covered entirely by a great blanket of ice, in places nearly five kilometres thick. The Arctic, however, is surrounded by the northern parts of Alaska, Canada, Greenland, Norway and the USSR. Consequently, it is better known for its large mammals, such as the polar bear, musk ox and reindeer.

Rafting around the Arctic

THERE are about 20,000 polar bears living in the Arctic. There were once many more, but they have been hunted for sport and for their valuable skins. These days the bears are protected and can safely travel all around their northern home in the Arctic. Some individuals even move backwards and forwards between Alaska or Scandinavia and the USSR, quite oblivious to political boundaries.

Polar bears can sometimes be seen floating hundreds or thousands of kilometres out to sea on ice floes, which they use like rafts. They love to travel and often set off on these journeys with no particular place to go.

Apart from scientists – representing no fewer than twelve different countries – there are no people living permanently in the Antarctic. But many parts of the Arctic are inhabited. Perhaps the best known Arctic inhabitants are the 50,000 eskimos living around the coast of Greenland.

Life without light

WHEN it is summer in the Arctic it is winter in the Antarctic – and vice versa – but in both cases there is very little difference between night and day.

The angle of the earth is such that, at the poles, the sun is always shining during summer but it almost disappears during winter. This means that animals and plants living in either the Arctic or the Antarctic have to be able to cope with almost continuous daylight for much of the year and prolonged darkness for months on end during the remainder.

So when the Arctic is experiencing an endless day, the Antarctic is experiencing an endless night.

Elephant seal

The biggest elephant seals are much taller than a man when they rear up and lift their heads in the air. They can be six metres long and weigh nearly four tonnes. Their name comes from the male seal's enormous nose, which is so long it overhangs his mouth. It is used as a loudspeaker to amplify the animal's threatening roars, which can be heard from several kilometres away.

Survival in the cold

ONE of the main difficulties associated with living in either the Arctic or the Antarctic is the cold weather. The temperature in polar regions never rises much above 10 degrees centigrade and, particularly in the winter, often falls far below this. In some areas it may reach minus 60 degrees centigrade or less.

Polar animals have to be able to keep warm, and have found many different ways to do this. For example, emperor penguins take it in turns to stand on the inside of their 'rookeries' where it is warmest; musk ox and polar bears have dense fur to protect them from the arctic cold; and whales have a thick layer of blubber beneath the skin.

There are some animals, however, which cannot live in such cold conditions. These are the cold-blooded creatures, such as snakes, lizards and frogs, whose body temperatures are always more or less the same as the temperatures outside. If these are too low their bodies simply cannot work.

The hottest and coldest places on earth

Coldest:
Pole of Cold, Antarctica
averages −57.8°C

Hottest:
Dallol, Ethiopia
averages +34.4°C

Most extreme:
Verkhoyansk, Siberia
from −70°C to + 36.7°C

Lapland bunting
Lapland buntings are sparrow-sized birds which can fly very well but rarely spend much of their time in the air. They prefer to eat, nest and sleep on the ground.

Nevertheless, technology is allowing modern man to invade further and further into these far-flung regions of the world. The pressure on the poles – in the constant search for oil and mineral reserves, from the hunting of whales, seals and penguins and even through dumping things in their seas – is increasing all the time.

In the spring, snow geese fly north to the Arctic tundra to breed. They spend the winter months in places like the Southern United States and Mexico.

The world traveller

IN its lifetime, an arctic tern flies far enough to travel to the moon and back. Every year – for up to thirty years – it migrates from one end of the world to the other and back again, a total distance of up to 40,000 kilometres. This is probably the longest migration undertaken by any bird in the world – and often means staying in the air for no fewer than eight months out of every twelve. Many individuals spend the southern summer in the Antarctic and move north, for the northern summer, to breed in the Arctic.

When the nesting season is over, the male and female terns split up before embarking on the return journey south. They do not see one another again for nearly a year, until it is time to meet – in the same colony – the following season.

Living under the ice

IF you stand on sea ice in the Antarctic you may be lucky enough to hear Weddell seals calling to one another underneath. They live further south than any other seal, in areas where the sea is often frozen for eight months of the year to a depth of several metres.

In the Antarctic winter Weddell seals spend most of their time in the water. They are the deepest divers of all seals. The record-holder once dived to a depth of 600 metres and didn't come up to breathe for 73 minutes. Perfectly adapted to living in the eerie world under the

Snowshoe hare
As the seasons change, the snowshoe hare changes colour to match its surroundings. In the summer it is brown and looks like any other hare. But in the winter it is white, making it very difficult for foxes and other predators to see it against the snow.

THE POLES
DID YOU KNOW?

Weddell seals can stay underwater for over an hour and are able to dive to 300 metres or more below the surface.

There are no penguins in the Arctic.

A blue whale may eat up to three or more tonnes of krill – a tiny shrimp-like creature – in one go. It simply swims through shoals of the animals with its huge mouth open, taking in gulps of the 'krill soup'.

The thickest ice in the world is in the Antarctic where, in some places, it can be nearly five kilometres thick.

The largest iceberg ever measured was found in the Antarctic in 1956. 335 kilometres long and 97 kilometres wide, it was bigger than Belgium.

It is thought that over 100 million birds, including penguins, petrels, skuas (left) and albatrosses, breed around the shores and islands of Antarctica every year.

ice, their eyes are very large to help them see in the murky depths; and their front teeth stick out, so they can gnaw through the frozen surface when they need to breathe.

When a pair of adelie penguins are courting, the male offers a stone to the female. If she bows and accepts it, he knows that he has found his mate.

ANIMAL KINGDOM CLASSIFICATION

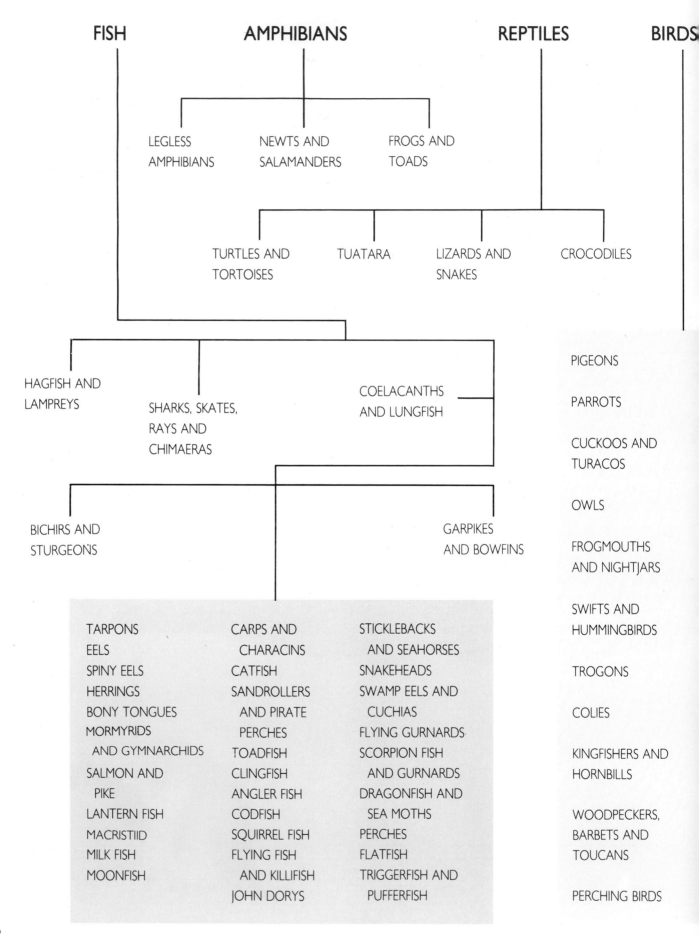

FISH AMPHIBIANS REPTILES BIRDS

LEGLESS AMPHIBIANS

NEWTS AND SALAMANDERS

FROGS AND TOADS

TURTLES AND TORTOISES

TUATARA

LIZARDS AND SNAKES

CROCODILES

PIGEONS

HAGFISH AND LAMPREYS

COELACANTHS AND LUNGFISH

PARROTS

SHARKS, SKATES, RAYS AND CHIMAERAS

CUCKOOS AND TURACOS

OWLS

BICHIRS AND STURGEONS

GARPIKES AND BOWFINS

FROGMOUTHS AND NIGHTJARS

SWIFTS AND HUMMINGBIRDS

TARPONS
EELS
SPINY EELS
HERRINGS
BONY TONGUES
MORMYRIDS
 AND GYMNARCHIDS
SALMON AND
 PIKE
LANTERN FISH
MACRISTIID
MILK FISH
MOONFISH

CARPS AND
 CHARACINS
CATFISH
SANDROLLERS
 AND PIRATE
 PERCHES
TOADFISH
CLINGFISH
ANGLER FISH
CODFISH
SQUIRREL FISH
FLYING FISH
 AND KILLIFISH
JOHN DORYS

STICKLEBACKS
 AND SEAHORSES
SNAKEHEADS
SWAMP EELS AND
 CUCHIAS
FLYING GURNARDS
SCORPION FISH
 AND GURNARDS
DRAGONFISH AND
 SEA MOTHS
PERCHES
FLATFISH
TRIGGERFISH AND
 PUFFERFISH

TROGONS

COLIES

KINGFISHERS AND HORNBILLS

WOODPECKERS, BARBETS AND TOUCANS

PERCHING BIRDS

MAMMALS   INVERTEBRATES

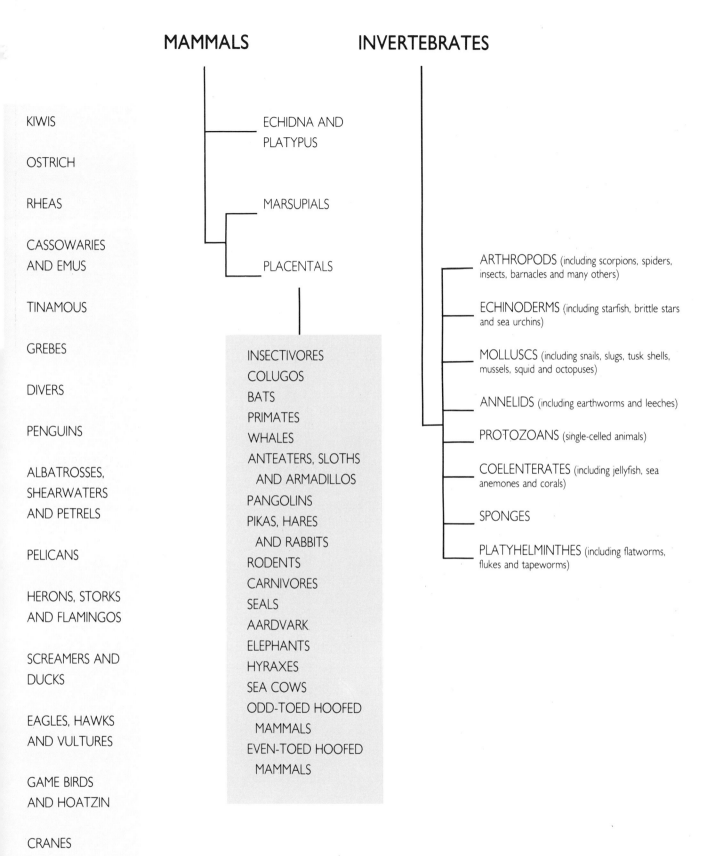

KIWIS

OSTRICH

RHEAS

CASSOWARIES
AND EMUS

TINAMOUS

GREBES

DIVERS

PENGUINS

ALBATROSSES,
SHEARWATERS
AND PETRELS

PELICANS

HERONS, STORKS
AND FLAMINGOS

SCREAMERS AND
DUCKS

EAGLES, HAWKS
AND VULTURES

GAME BIRDS
AND HOATZIN

CRANES

WADERS, GULLS
AND AUKS

ECHIDNA AND
PLATYPUS

MARSUPIALS

PLACENTALS

INSECTIVORES
COLUGOS
BATS
PRIMATES
WHALES
ANTEATERS, SLOTHS
    AND ARMADILLOS
PANGOLINS
PIKAS, HARES
    AND RABBITS
RODENTS
CARNIVORES
SEALS
AARDVARK
ELEPHANTS
HYRAXES
SEA COWS
ODD-TOED HOOFED
    MAMMALS
EVEN-TOED HOOFED
    MAMMALS

ARTHROPODS (including scorpions, spiders,
insects, barnacles and many others)

ECHINODERMS (including starfish, brittle stars
and sea urchins)

MOLLUSCS (including snails, slugs, tusk shells,
mussels, squid and octopuses)

ANNELIDS (including earthworms and leeches)

PROTOZOANS (single-celled animals)

COELENTERATES (including jellyfish, sea
anemones and corals)

SPONGES

PLATYHELMINTHES (including flatworms,
flukes and tapeworms)

Please note: This is not strictly a taxonomical classification. Some groups have been sub-
divided further than others because they contain more familiar animals.

GLOSSARY

Adaptation
A part or feature of a living thing that helps it to survive in a particular environment, such as the thick woolly coat of an arctic fox that helps it to keep warm in freezing cold weather

Animal
Any living thing except a plant or a fungus; technically, a living thing that cannot make its own food (as plants do); most animals can move around voluntarily

Aquatic
Living in water

Arboreal
Living in trees

Camouflage
Any form of disguise used by a living thing to blend in with the background and thereby hide from its predators or prey

Carnivore
An animal or plant that feeds on other animals, or mostly on other animals; there is also a group of animals, known as the Carnivores, that includes dogs, cats, hyenas, bears and raccoons

Common
In wildlife terms, occuring in large numbers or regularly

Conservation
To protect and preserve something; wildlife conservation involves protecting and conserving natural areas with all their resident animals and plants; the word 'conservation' is also applied to the use of animals, plants and other natural resources in such a way as to improve the quality of life for mankind — but without wasting or using up those resources

Continent
Any of the main large land areas of the earth, such as North America, Asia or Australia

Desert
A dry, sandy region with little plant (or animal) life; strictly speaking, an area with a particularly low rainfall

Distribution
The areas, or parts of the world, in which an animal or plant is found

Diurnal
Active during daylight

Endangered species
An animal or plant in danger of becoming extinct

Environment
All the surroundings of a living thing, including other animals and plants, the soil, the climate and so on

Evolution
The gradual change with time of living things. Animals and plants are always changing to become better adapted to their environment; since the environment is also changing, evolution is a continuing process

Extinct
A species of animal or plant which is no longer living and has therefore died out completely; officially, a species becomes extinct if there have been no certain records of it for 50 years; the dodo is one of the best known of all extinct species

Habitat
The type of place where an animal or plant lives, such as a lake, a wood or a desert

Herbivore
An animal that eats only, or mostly, plants

Herd
A group of large animals (such as wildebeest or buffalo) living, feeding or migrating together

Hibernation
A period of inactivity, during very cold or generally bad weather, when an animal's body temperature, pulse rate and breathing rate all fall

Intelligence
The ability to learn or understand new things from experience

Invertebrate
An animal without a backbone

Jungle
The popular term for tropical rain forest; land with a dense growth of trees, vines etc. in the tropics

Mammal
Any animal in a group of vertebrates whose young are fed with their mother's milk. Mammals are warm blooded and breathe air; most have fur on their bodies

Marine
Living in the sea

Marsupial
A group of mammals, most of which have pouches in which to keep their young in safety, found in North and South America and Australasia, such as kangaroos, opossums and bandicoots

Migration
A regular journey, usually linked to the seasons, when animals move from one place to another to feed or breed

Nature reserve	An area of land set aside for the conservation of animals, plants and their habitats; it is usually legally protected against other uses
Nocturnal	Active during darkness
Omnivore	An animal that eats both plants and other animals
Population	A group of animals or plants of the same species which are fairly separate from other such groups
Predator	The hunter: an animal that kills other animals for food
Prey	The hunted: an animal that is killed and eaten by another animal
Pride	A group or family of lions; a pride may include as many as six adult males and even more lionesses and cubs – perhaps 25 animals in all
Rare	Uncommon; not often seen or found
Solitary	Living alone. An example is the tiger, which only meets another tiger to mate
Species	A group of living things (not necessarily living together) that look similar and can breed successfully
Sub-species	A sub-group of living things belonging to the same species but usually restricted to a certain area, such as an island or a mountain, and differing in some way from other such sub-groups
Terrestrial	Living on land
Territory	An area 'owned' by an animal or group of animals, which is defended against other members of the same species when they try to intrude
Tropical	In or from the tropics, the part of the world on either side of the equator between the Tropic of Cancer and the Tropic of Capricorn
Tundra	The vast, nearly level, treeless areas of land in the arctic regions
Vertebrate	An animal with a backbone

Bearded seal

INDEX